ArtScroll Series®

Rabbi Nosson Scherman / Rabbi Meir Zlotowitz

General Editors

She Shall

The faith and courage of extraordinary women

Published by

Mesorah Publications, ltd

Be Praised

by Avraham Erlanger
Translated by Libby Lazewnik

FIRST EDITION
First Impression … July 1999
Second Impression … October 1999
Third Impression … July 2001
Fourth Impression … July 2009

Published and Distributed by
MESORAH PUBLICATIONS, LTD.
4401 Second Avenue / Brooklyn, N.Y 11232

Distributed in Europe by
LEHMANNS
Unit E, Viking Business Park
Rolling Mill Road
Jarow, Tyne & Wear, NE32 3DP
England

Distributed in Australia and New Zealand
by **GOLDS WORLDS OF JUDAICA**
3-13 William Street
Balaclava, Melbourne 3183
Victoria, Australia

Distributed in Israel by
SIFRIATI / A. GITLER — BOOKS
6 Hayarkon Street
Bnei Brak 51127

Distributed in South Africa by
KOLLEL BOOKSHOP
Ivy Common
105 William Road
Norwood 2192, Johannesburg, South Africa

ISBN 10: 1-57819-450-4 / ISBN 13: 978-1-57819-450-6 (hard cover)
ISBN 10: 1-57819-451-2 / ISBN 13: 978-1-57819-451-3 (paperback)

Typography by CompuScribe at ArtScroll Studios, Ltd.

Printed in the United States of America by Noble Book Press Corp.
Bound by Sefercraft, Quality Bookbinders, Ltd., Brooklyn N.Y. 11232

Table of Contents

❧ Foreword

MANY TALES HAVE BEEN TOLD ABOUT JEWISH women, whose spiritual valor has formed the bedrock upon which our nation was founded. The following stories were written piece by piece; many originally appeared in biographies published by the subject's descendants. The notion of collecting them into a single book was considered a timely one. No one reading about the greatness of these righteous women — women spanning the spectrum of Judaism — can fail to be inspired.

The stories are arranged by topic: prayer, sacrifice, faith, love of Torah, lovingkindness and others, arising from the lives of these valiant women in recent generations. In the course of assembling this collection, we insisted on utilizing only the most reliable of sources. In quoting from the original stories, we attempted, wherever possible, to remain true to the original manuscript. Where oral interviews by family members came into play, their thoughts have been rendered in clear, concise language, understandable to all.

Obviously, the available material far exceeds the amount of space available to us on these pages. Additional stories will follow, please G-d, in future volumes. Apart from the ones we have gathered in our own files, tales keep pouring in from the public — stories that will, we are certain, immeasurably enrich our lives as well as our perspectives.

Our gratitude must go to all those families who have shared this wonderful material with us, and to the rabbis and educators who encouraged the publication of this work, stressing its importance for our time. In essence, it is they who blazed the path along which this book has traveled.

Our thanks, too, go to all those who read and critiqued the material, and especially to my dear brother-in-law who carefully reviewed all the material in this book.

Our acknowledgements must also extend to the committee members appointed by the *Beis Din* of Rav Nissim Karelitz *shlita*, who perused every page to ensure its suitability for the Jewish public — and, in so doing, exhibited a remarkable understanding of the reader's heart.

My wife, Batya, contributed greatly of her wisdom, ideas, and practical assistance in every stage of this work. Whatever light and beauty this book enjoys is largely due to her.

I must not omit a mention of my dear children, who served as my first motivation in putting together this book, and who infused it with life.

Many thanks to my father-in-law, Rabbi Chaim Yitzchak *shlita*, and his wife, Rebbetzin Esther, for their generous assistance. It is impossible to overestimate their influence on our family, both spiritually and physically. May they continue their blessed work in good health for many years to come.

Last, my dear parents, Rabbi Akiva and Tzipporah Rochel, who were unstinting in their efforts to build their home on the twin premises of Torah and *chesed*. The fruits of this book's labor have their source in those wonderful roots.

May it be Hashem's will that this book attain all the lofty aims with which it was conceived.

Avraham Erlanger

Part One:
Shabbos Lights

❧ A Tower of Strength

I T WAS FRIDAY NIGHT IN THE HOME OF THE *TZADDIK* of Jerusalem Reb Aryeh Levine. His wife, Tzipporah Chanah, sat near the flickering candles, *davening* softly. An enchanting purity shone from her face as she covered her eyes with her hands. "One who hasn't seen the Rebbetzin *davening* doesn't really knows what *davening* is," members of her household had been known to remark. This time, the Rebbetzin was murmuring a tearful prayer for her youngest son, who was critically ill.

The boy lay in a corner of the room. His body was skeletal, his face pale as the sheet that covered him. In anguish and pleading, the mother beseeched Heaven for his speedy recovery.

In the world outside, World War One was raging. Many perished in the famine that held *Eretz Yisrael* in its deathly grip. Scores of children were dying every day in epidemics that swept like wildfire from house to house. One of these illnesses had infected the Levine child.

From time to time, the Rebbetzin went to the bed and tenderly attended to her son's needs. With her last pennies she had purchased a bit of goat's milk, which she fed to the small boy, one tiny spoonful at a time.

But the illness refused to give up its hold on the young body. If anything, its ravages grew stronger. The doctor, summoned in haste on this Shabbos night, whispered sadly, "There's nothing more to be done. Only Hashem can help now."

On Shabbos morning, the boy's soul returned to its Maker.

The mother stood by her son's bed, biting her lips. No! She would not weep — not on Shabbos. She would restrain her grief, bottle it up so that not a drop spilled out on this day. Summoning all her considerable strength of character, the Rebbetzin urged a similar fortitude on her family. She comforted and encouraged them, reminding them over and over that today was Shabbos!

The usual *zemiros* resounded through the house that day. When a neighbor came tapping at her door, the Rebbetzin answered pleasantly, betraying no sign of the tragedy. How could she distress her neighbors on Shabbos?

Only when the day had waned into night, when the stars emerged to replace the sun in a navy velvet sky, did the mother give way to her grief. Only then did she allow herself to mourn her beloved little boy, taken from her that morning.

This was not the first child the Levines had lost. Three others had been taken from them during the war, either through sickness or famine. Always, Reb Aryeh and his wife sought to accept the judgment that had been passed on them. "Hashem gives, Hashem takes away, may Hashem's Name be blessed," the Rebbetzin would say, more to strengthen her family than to comfort herself. But it was so very difficult to find solace over the death of her youngest, her Avraham Binyamin, snatched away at the tender age of just 1½ years.

He had been a wonder child. Everyone who saw him predicted greatness in his future. At his birth, the entire house seemed infused with light. He began to talk when he was just a few months old. At a very young age, he displayed the extraordinary understanding of a much older child. Those who heard him speak were often stunned, disbelieving the evidence of their own ears. When he was 9 month old, he would recite the *"Shehakol"* blessing with simple purity before tasting his mother's milk.

The taste of joy was sweet, but all too brief. The treasure granted to Reb Aryeh and his wife was taken back after just a year and a half. As the couple sat *shivah* for their beloved son, two women, both new immigrants, appeared at the door. They had come to console the Rebbetzin.

They found her immersed in prayer. With a face as tranquil as an angel's, wearing an expression of devotion and deep emotion, she poured out her heart to her Creator. The women watched her, astonished and awed: They had never heard such prayer before. Her serenity, during these days of deepest mourning, impressed them profoundly.

"How can she do it?" one of them murmured to the other in their native tongue. "How can she remain so sane?"

Her friend nodded. "You're right. I've never seen a woman so calm during her *shivah* week."

The Rebbetzin completed her *tefillah*, but the visitors continued whispering about her. They spoke Russian, a language which they assumed she did not know. It was a mistaken assumption. Though she chose not to flaunt the fact, the Rebbetzin was fluent in many languages. Russian was one of them. She listened to the women talk.

"Sane?" she responded at last, very softly. "My dear women, I am simply accepting, with love, what has been decreed for me. Had I been worthy, my darling son would have learned one day in an earthly yeshivah; since I am not worthy, he will learn instead in the Heavenly one."

In silence, the visitors bowed their heads. Now they

understood who the woman sitting before them really was. The knowledge robbed them — literally — of the power of speech.

Quite simply, they had never before encountered such greatness in their lives.

✒ The Miracle

Ollendorf, Germany. The skies were leaden, the winds strong and fitful. The trees were shedding their leaves at a rapid rate, so that streets newly swept had to be swept again. Leaves and bits of litter danced haphazardly on the wind's back.

It was a dismal scene, certainly not one calculated to warm the broken hearts of the Jewish prisoners working in the munitions factory. About a thousand Jewish women labored there. Supervision was constant and harsh. From time to time a female S.S. supervisor would make a surprise inspection; these visits usually ended in heavy punishments for us.

On this gray autumn day, a piece of exciting information was whispered in my ear.

"I've gotten hold of candles — Shabbos candles. Do you want to light them, Miriam?"

I stared at my friend. She smiled, saying, "Don't you believe me? Shabbos candles! I found some wax in the department where I work. I melted it down in one of these boxes — and here they are. Shabbos candles!"

My heart soared. Shabbos lights, in the very midst of the darkness that pressed in on us from every side! In the center of the arctic menace, a tiny pinpoint of light and warmth — the Shabbos flames.

In that instant, I forgot the S.S., forgot instruction manuals, arms and missiles, forgot the cold and the whips and the starvation rations. I forgot the image of the loaded gun that was never far from my inner eye. In short, I forgot where I was. The whispered secret I had just heard had the power to spirit away the ugly munitions factory and everything in it.

"Well?" my friend asked. "Do you want to light the candles?"

"Yes!"

"Aren't you afraid?"

"Afraid — of what?"

"The whip, the gun, the gas chamber — "

I cut her off. "I'm afraid of the stick in the hand of my Father in Heaven. I intend to fulfill my obligations as a Jewish woman."

That night, my friend smuggled her treasure to me. There were two simple candles, concealed in a long cylinder. I clutched them to my heart, feeling almost as if I had found my lost child, snatched out of my arms many days before — as if I had found a portion of my own heart that they had stolen away.

What power did those candles have? How were they were able to ignite such a flame inside me? I had no explanation. I only knew that I sensed the souls of all the righteous women through the ages reaching out to me through those candles. Perhaps, too, I saw my mother's covered face, and felt her spirit illuminate my subdued and broken heart.

I hid the candles in my bag — a collection of rags, actually, in which I occasionally managed to store a crust of bread for some sick friend. There were still two days until Shabbos, two days of unremitting gloom. But those two days seemed infused with the light to come — the light of Shabbos. At last I understood our Sages' words: *"Zachor es yom haShabbos"* — Remember the Shabbos, remember it every day. If you come across some delicacy that will not spoil, buy it in honor of the Shabbos. I had no delicacy, no special food for Shabbos, but I had something very valuable indeed — my holy Shabbos candles.

Friday came. In my room, 14 Jewish girls had completed the day's work and were preparing to welcome the Shabbos Queen. The room was unfurnished except for a single old chest and our cots. I placed the candles atop the chest. I wanted to give all my friends the opportunity to share in my *mitzvah* by answering *"Amen."*

The time for candlelighting approached. It was the lovely hour before sunset; the western skies were already stained crimson and purple. Today it seemed seven times more beautiful than usual, as though the sun itself had decided to adorn our room in honor of the Shabbos before sinking out of sight. A ray of sunlight wandered into the room and rested for a moment on the candles. It lent them a golden glow, making the simple homemade candles seem taller, nobler. Even as I trembled, the ray trembled, too, and moved on.

Thirteen pairs of eyes fixed themselves on me. Some of them reflected the fear we all shared — the fear that the enemy would intrude on our precious sanctuary. But every eye shone with the fire that had been kindled in every heart. Each one of us knew how closely her own being was bound with the lighting of those candles. We were ready for anything.

I stepped up to the candles. "Just like my mother used to do," I heard someone whisper behind me. I sensed rather than saw the way the others nodded their heads, their throats choked with tears.

I struck a match, and lit the candles.

I passed my hands over the candles and was about to bring my fingertips to my eyes when, suddenly, heavy footsteps sounded in the corridor. We recognized those footsteps. They belonged to our S.S. supervisor. Our hearts stopped.

Quickly, I covered my eyes and recited the blessing. "Blessed are You … to light the Shabbos candle." I remained where I was, hands over my eyes, pleading in a strange, strangled voice, "Master of the Universe, You know that I did not do this for my own pleasure or honor. I did it to honor You, to honor the holy Shabbos, so that everyone would remember that You created the world in six days and rested on the seventh."

The supervisor flung open the door. With a single glance she took in the entire scene. We all stood frozen in a silence that seemed shatterproof. As I continued praying with covered eyes, she stood silent, astounded.

When I removed my hands, I heard her issue a sharp order. "Go outside to the waiting truck!"

The other girls hurried to obey her command, with the S.S. woman following close behind. I was left alone in the room. I looked at the candles. "Will my lighting these candles lead to all my friends being carted away to who-knows-where?" I wondered, near despair.

The flames burned brightly as my lips moved in soundless prayer. I felt as though all of history's good women were bearing my prayers directly to the Holy Throne. And then peace returned, and I knew with certainty: My friends would not be harmed because of these holy candles.

Slowly, I walked outside to join the others. A short distance away, I saw the parked truck. I tentatively made my way toward it. Just as I arrived, my friends appeared from behind the truck, bearing loaves of bread.

Their faces were serene as they explained, "She ordered us to take these loaves to the kitchen."

Uncontrollably, I burst out in words of thanks and praise. "Blessed is He Who performed a miracle for me on this spot!" As the sages taught, "The messengers of a *mitzvah* are truly not harmed."

I lifted my eyes heavenward. The sun had not yet sunk beneath the rim of the horizon. A last stripe of light lingered at the western edge of the sky, as though to proclaim the miracle. Then, its job finished, it disappeared — and the Shabbos Queen descended on the world.

❧ I Will Never Forget

Yehudis was forced to make the trip from her native town of Orlov to the death camp, knowing full well the journey's implications, but bearing the knowledge with grace and fortitude. Only with such an attitude, she felt, could she perform as many *mitzvos* as possible and cling ever closer to her Creator — her primary motivation in all she did.

Yehudis's dignity stood revealed from the moment she arrived at the camp. Every morning, she drank only a small portion of her allotted drink and used the rest to ritually wash her hands. She saved a measure of her daily bread to barter for a small *siddur,* from which she whispered her supplications to the Master of the Universe, and which she loaned to friends.

For some time before Pesach, Yehudis and her friends began to save bits of potato, in order to be able to subsist on the festival without eating *chametz.* On Yom Kippur, they hid their bread rations until nightfall. When the Nazis heard that these girls were fasting, they confiscated the reserved bread so that the girls were forced to fast not one, but two consecutive days.

Yehudis — daughter of Rabbi Avraham Yehoshua Ratek, may his blood be avenged — staunchly refused to work on Shabbos at any price. Though many of the other girls were taken out and killed for taking such a stand, her single-mindedness in this area was astonishing. She offered to work a double shift on weekdays instead.

When a truck came to transport inmates from place to place, and it appeared as though the trip would afford opportunity for escape, Yehudis refused to go as it involved traveling on Shabbos. She remained behind in the camp. In her heart, she clung to the promise that had been made to her by the *Tzaddik* of Orlov — a promise that she would be saved in the merit of her Shabbos observance. That decision became the linchpin of her eventual rescue.

Her job involved the preparation of bombs for the Nazi war machine. These bombs weighed up to 70 kilos, or more than 150 pounds each. It was backbreaking labor. But as she worked, Yehudis would in her pleasant voice sing a Yiddish song entitled *"G-tt Is Gerecht"* — G-d Is Just. The chorus of this song may be translated as follows: "G-d, Your decrees are just. The Creator knows what He is doing, knows what He is doing. No one is punished for naught."

Her rescue from the Holocaust came about as a result of her Shabbos observance: The death transports were carried out on Shabbos, the day on which Yehudis did not work.

Upon her arrival in Switzerland, she married the *tzaddik,* Rabbi Chaim Aryeh Erlanger. During her last days, as she lay on her deathbed, Yehudis lifted her hands — trembling and almost transparent from the suffering of her final illness — and sang out loud, *"G-tt is gerecht"* … G-d is just …

❧ The Accident

The following story is found in the book *Melachim Amunayich:*

A child was crossing the street when he was struck by a car. He was rushed, critically injured, to the hospital's intensive care unit.

During the police investigation into the matter, the driver of the vehicle testified that the boy had darted unexpectedly into the road, affording him insufficient time to apply the brakes. Still, his conscience troubled him. He visited the child in the hospital, his heart wrung in compassion for the anxious family. "How can I atone for what I did? Though the fault was not mine, I was the one who caused these injuries. What can I do?"

The driver expected the family to demand a hefty financial recompense. To his astonishment, this was far from what was requested.

Sitting at her son's bedside, the boy's mother said quietly, "If you want to help my son, and to help all of us, take it upon yourself to observe the Shabbos. In that merit, the boy will recover! We are all responsible for one another. Shabbos is the source of blessing. When the blessing of Shabbos begins to shower upon you, some of it will surely flow our way."

The driver heard her plea, tears flowing unchecked down his face. On the spot, he decided to accept the woman's suggestion. He would study the laws of Shabbos and draw closer to his Maker.

True to his resolution, he began to study in a yeshivah several hours a week. He observed the holy Shabbos. With the passage of time, he became engaged to a fine Jewish girl with whom he glowingly made plans to establish a true Jewish home.

The child he had inadvertently struck with his car recovered and grew strong again — and was the guest who danced with the most joyous abandon at that very special wedding.

Part Two:
Al Kiddush Hashem

✿ Solika

THERE IS A GRAVE IN THE CEMETERY AT FEZ, Morocco, that is the final resting place of Solika — or, as the Moroccan Jews call her, "Holy Solika." The grave, situated close by those of R' Yehudah ben Attar and R' Avner Sarfati, draws numerous visitors, who come to pray there and to beseech Heaven in that righteous girl's merit. The tombstone reads: "The *tzadekes* Solika Hajiwval."

Who was she? And what was the greatness that merited her such honor?

The Hajuval family lived in the city of Tangiers. The father was a pious and G-d-fearing man who dealt honestly in business matters. He and his wife had a daughter who was blessed with everything a parent's heart could desire: a kindly disposition, pleasant manners and a beautiful face. When the father would praise her by saying, *"Kol kevudah bas melech penimah"* ("The glory of a king's daughter is within"), Solika would answer, "The less I venture out into the street, the better for all of us." Indeed, she refrained from leaving home as much as possible, and carried her father's message close to her heart.

Still, it was necessary at times to go out. On one such occasion, a Moslem neighbor saw her and was instantly smitten with her beauty. She, and no other, must be his wife!

Islamic law did not favor him. By the tenets of that faith, a Moslem could not marry a Jewess unless she converted to his religion. One day, the young man's father knocked on the Hajuvals' door with an extraordinary request. In order for his son to be able to wed Solika, he asked that she agree to convert to Islam!

The visit came as a thunderbolt to the Jewish family. Their neighbor was a powerful man — a man who would not rest until he achieved what he desired. They tried to explain that it was impossible to accede to his request, as it ran counter to their own faith; but he would not be deterred.

In the dead of night, the family removed Solika from her home and smuggled her into the concealment of a warehouse. When the Sultan's soldiers came looking for her, the parents informed them sadly that their daughter had run away from home.

A thorough search of the Hajuval house ascertained that the girl was not there. The soldiers, however, did not believe that she had run away. They seized Solika's mother and bore her off to jail in the daughter's place.

When Solika heard the news, she was devastated. How could she permit her mother to languish in prison because of her? With head held high and a resolute stride, she turned herself in to the authorities — maintaining all the while that she would never convert. She was thrown into jail, and her mother was released.

On the appointed day, Solika was taken to court to face the charges against her. She was appalled to learn that her wealthy neighbor had accused her of having converted to Islam and then reneged: a grave sin in Moslem eyes. The judges ruled that she must return to the Islamic faith — on pain of death.

Solika stood proud and brave before the judges, and announced, "I have never converted to Islam. I was born a Jew, and a Jew I will remain. Neither torture nor death will make me change my mind. I am prepared to die in the sanctification of G-d's Name, rather than turn my back on my fathers' faith."

Even the judges were moved by her courage. Never before had they encountered someone prepared to sacrifice her life rather than betray her faith. Judgment was postponed, and Solika returned to her cell.

As the days passed and she remained adamant in her refusal to convert, the judges decided to transfer her to the city of Fez. The Sultan's palace was located there. That was also the place where — with the Sultan's stamp of approval — prisoners were taken out to be executed.

As it happened, when Solika arrived in Fez one of the Sultan's sons saw her and desired to take her as a wife. He promised her riches and honor if she would only agree to abandon her religion. But Solika stood firm. Neither gold nor silver nor all the Sultan's glory could measure up to the value of her faith in her G-d and His holy Torah. "Nothing," she declared, "could make me betray my people and my faith."

The prince, seeing her so determined, hurried to the chief rabbi of Fez, with the following ultimatum. The Rabbi was to persuade Solika to convert to Islam, or all the city's Jews — indeed, all of Morocco's Jews — would suffer bitterly.

The Rabbi went to Solika's cell. He tested the strength of her faith and witnessed its purity, deriving courage from her own pure heart. It was this that gave her the will to cling steadfast to her position.

"Are you any different from Queen Esther?" the Rabbi asked wearily. "Didn't she marry King Achashverosh in order to save her people?"

"Yes," Solika answered. "But Esther did not abandon her faith. It says in the Megillah that Esther did not reveal that she was Jewish — an option that is closed to me. I have been asked to convert. Am I to abandon G-d's word?" And, once again, she repeated, "I am prepared to die *al kiddush Hashem,* for the sanctification of G-d's Name — just so I remain a Jew!"

The Rabbi left her cell in tears.

Shortly thereafter, Solika's fate was sealed.

Minutes before her execution, the prince came to Solika and pleaded, "Just picture your happiness when you embrace Islam. You will rule over all of Morocco. All the world's beauty will be open to you — "

Solika was engrossed in her final preparations for departing this world and entering the next. She made a silent *viduy,* a confession of her sins, and steeled herself in the armor of her faith to face her ordeal. The prince's words hardly registered. Without a single cry, devotedly murmuring the words of *Shema Yisrael,* Solika submitted to her awful decree.

She returned her soul to its Maker in purity and holiness, and earned the title of "Holy Solika" forever after. Buried among the righteous in the Fez cemetery, she became a symbol of *kedushah* and modesty, self-sacrifice and love of Hashem — and her grave the symbol of hope for the many who come to pray for salvation in the merit of Solika.

❧ The Blood Libel

This story took place 300 years ago, in the city of Drobitch, and it happened to a wonderful woman named Aidel, the married daughter of Reb Moshe Kiknish.

A Gentile maidservant hid the corpse of a Christian child in Aidel's house on Pesach night, for the purpose of creating a blood libel. Under police interrogation, the maid testified that she had murdered the child on her mistress's orders, to serve the needs of the Jewish community.

This libel nearly brought total destruction on the community. Aidel calculated: "If I deny the story, the entire community will be killed or otherwise harmed. But if I 'confess' that it was my hand alone that perpetrated the deed, only I will sacrifice my life, and the rest will be saved."

Accordingly, Aidel told the police that the order had issued from her lips, but that her people were innocent of any guilt in the matter. She was sentenced to death.

Hearing this, the maidservant had a change of heart. Remorse for what she had done to her mistress gnawed at her conscience. Finally, she stood up in court and testified that she had lied — that her mistress had played no part in the death of the Christian child.

The judges rejected her testimony out of hand. The death sentence stood.

Influenced by the local priests, the authorities agreed to give Aidel one last chance to save her life: by conversion to Christianity. Many people came to urge this course upon her, but Aidel was staunch in her faith. She would not convert. She would die as a Jew.

Her execution was scheduled for a Friday.

The day came — *Erev Shabbos kodesh.* Aidel dressed in her Shabbos clothes, lit the Shabbos candles and recited the blessing over them with a heart overflowing with joy. Then she went to the execution house, where bales of hay were heaped around her and ignited. Lifting her hands Heavenward, Aidel's soul ascended with the leaping flames.

With the waning of the sun, just before Shabbos, the city turned out to bury her with full honors, amid a profound acknowledgement of the woman's limitless devotion to her people and her G-d.

❧ The Heroic "93"

The Jewish world was awed and shaken by the valor of 93 Bais Yaakov girls in Cracow, who gave their lives to avoid defilement by the evil Nazi S.S. Much was made of the story in the press at the time, but there was never a full accounting, with all its details.

Subsequently, a letter was received from one of the Cracow Bais Yaakov girls who was an eyewitness to the episode, right up to its final moments. It is our obligation — and our honor — to print that letter here in its entirety.

Bogota, Columbia 24 Nisan 5707 (1947)

To the Honored A. Chernesky:

As a student of your sister, Latza Wicherzh, at the Bais Yaakov of Cracow, and knowing that you reside in Tel Aviv, I feel obliged to send you the enclosed notebook. Some months ago I sent a copy of it to acquaintances in New York, but unfortunately have not yet received any response.

It is my hope that, please G-d, I will soon be rejoicing together with all my fellow Jews in our Holy Land. For various reasons I am forced to live here at the moment, and though I lack for nothing I long to be in Eretz Yisrael because, to my sorrow, I find no scope here for our idealistic work.

Are you well? Has any of your family survived? Out of my own extended family, I am grieved beyond words to report that hardly anyone is left except me.

My heart pains me because I have been left alive and did not merit joining my friends, teachers and parents in giving their lives for Hashem. Apparently, the sins of my youth kept me from that honor, and that causes me anguish. Still, I hope that all the travails I have suffered (I will not describe them in a letter) have erased my sins from the record.

I was with my friends until the last day. On that last bitter morning I was summoned suddenly to attend my ailing aunt. The next day, the old woman who cleaned the school told me that all the students and teachers had been moved to another house. I went there immediately to join them, but to my great distress the soldier guarding the gate refused me admittance. I hid near the house and listened to everything that was happening inside, until I burst into hysterical tears and the soldier chased me away.

Fighting broke out in Cracow then, lasting several weeks and preventing me from trying to give my friends and teachers a Jewish burial. After four weeks, I managed to leave Cracow disguised as a corpse. After many ordeals, I landed here in Bogota, far from my loved ones, both living and dead.

As an eyewitness, I feel obligated to send you details of the heroism of my friends — the girls and women of the Bais Yaakov of Cracow.

Do you have any word about your sister Latza? I would appreciate any news you can send me about our people in Eretz Yisrael.

Looking forward to hearing from you, and best regards,

The student of your sister,
Chana Weiss

The Bais Yaakov High School of Cracow stood like a lighthouse in the heart of the sea. In its classrooms, young Jewish girls absorbed the teachings of women steeped in faith, Torah learning and *mussar* — an army of women who had spread throughout the Diaspora to teach a generation of Jewish daughters adherence to Torah and observance of its *mitzvos*. The principal and teachers clung to the heritage bestowed on them by the mother of Bais Yaakov, Sarah Schenierer, transmitted her methods and her spirit to their students. The Bais Yaakov lent a nobility to the ancient Polish city.

War broke out. The enemy invaded Poland. Like beasts of prey, they fell upon the Jews, torturing and murdering them, defiling synagogues and Torah scrolls. Fathers were separated from their families, children were torn from their mothers. Young Jewish girls were defiled by the cruel oppressor. We were being punished in full measure for our sins.

A black cloud hung over the Bais Yaakov. It felt like perpetual night to the scores of girls who had gathered there from all parts of the country, far from their families, their parents, their brothers and sisters. Sorrow and pain emanated from their innocent eyes. Deep furrows etched themselves on the principal's and teachers' brows. Theirs was the responsibility for sustaining the girls in their care — both physically and spiritually. They must preserve their own serenity in the face of grave danger, and inculcate in the girls a faith in Hashem that would carry them through whatever was to come. Could they do it?

On the 12th day of Av 1942, after the initial period of turmoil, the girls and their teachers gathered in the large school auditorium. A silence akin to that which prevails during the recitation of *Kol Nidrei* hung over the room. The head principal spoke, her words breathing fire. This is what she said:

"My daughters! We *daven* each day, 'Do not bring us to the test.' But if the test does come upon us, we will pray for Hashem to strengthen our hearts, that we may withstand it.

"My dear daughters, I know the question that is pressing on your hearts: Why are these terrible misfortunes raining upon our holy brothers, our leaders and rabbis, on *chassidim* and other men of good deeds? We must remember what *Moshe Rabbeinu* said to *Bnei Yisrael* before his death: '*Ha-Tzur tamim po'alo ki kol derachav mishpat* — ' All of Hashem's work is perfect, because all of His paths are just. Hashem's ways are hidden from our understanding. We must be strong in our faith and our belief. Even if a sharp sword rests on a person's neck, he must not give up hope of mercy.

"My dear daughters! The time has come for you to demonstrate that you are prepared to practice what you've learned — that you are true to Hashem. The merit of our mothers, and of Sarah Schenierer, will help us stand up to the challenges we must face — "

Tears choked her throat. A soundless weeping swept through the ranks of students. No one was willing to shatter the trembling silence, the holy silence, that reigned in the vast hall.

Suddenly, heavy footsteps resounded. The door swung open, and in marched S.S. soldiers, their raucous laughter shattering the spell. One of them barked out an order, his voice booming like the roar of a jungle animal.

Ninety-three girls and women were taken to a house and crammed into four narrow rooms. The darkness made it impossible to see one another even up close. They had no idea of the time, or even whether it was day or night. They were beyond time. As the hours crept past, the girls listened to their teachers expound on the great *mitzvah* of dying *al kiddush Hashem* — for the sanctification of G-d's Name.

They spoke of Rabbi Akiva, whose skin was torn from him with metal combs, and who declared with his last breath, "All my life I've wondered when I might be able to fulfill the commandment, 'And you shall love the L-rd your G-d with all your heart and all your soul.'"

"We, too," said the teachers, "must accept this great

mitzvah — as we do all the *mitzvos* — with joy." The girls listened, and prepared to sanctify their G-d with love.

Their thoughts, however, were troubled. They were prepared to die for their faith — but what sort of death would the evil enemy choose for them? Shooting, or hanging, or burning? Would they be forced to leave this place — and if so, where would they go? One wish united them all: Let us be together. Let us never be separated! And if death be our decree, let us die together.

The door opened. The Nazis removed the girls in small groups to another dark room. The principal learned that the enemy was planning to try to draw the girls away from their faith.

The impact of this discovery on the principal and teachers was profound. They had been prepared for death, for torture, but their hope had been to give up their souls in purity. Never had they envisioned a catastrophe of such proportions — that the enemy would attempt to corrupt pure girls who had never known sin. Hashem was handing them a mighty test, the kind of test reserved for the great among the righteous. They would meet this one, too!

Ninety-three girls sat shoulder to shoulder in the dark rooms, shaking with cold and fear. But a fire burned in their hearts and their lips never stopped murmuring snatches of prayer and praises of Hashem. Indeed, their hearts were too full for the words their lips formed.

A deep sigh escaped one of the girls. It was a heartrending sigh, a sound that plumbed the depths of every soul in the room. A strained silence followed — broken by a single voice, quiet and proud. It was the principal:

"My dear daughters, *Chazal* taught us to pronounce the *berachah* of *Shehecheyanu* before performing a *mitzvah* that occurs only occasionally — such as *lulav*, *succah* and the festivals — because the essence of a man's life is observing the *mitzvos* and connecting to his Divine self. How much more so, when one merits fulfilling the *mitzvah* of giving up his entire physical life *al kiddush Hashem!* In other words, when he attains true, eternal life, he must pronounce the *Shehecheyanu* with even greater joy and meaning. We have had the merit to reach that place. We must thank Hashem.

"My dear daughters, are you not ready to give your lives for the sake of Hashem's *mitzvos,* through full awareness of what you are doing?"

With one voice, the girls answered, "We are ready!"

The tears flowed unchecked down the principal's face as she asked, in a choked voice, "Are you also prepared to suffer the tortures that might be inflicted on you — to suffer them with love?"

"We will try to withstand the worst tortures," the girls answered.

"My dear daughters, you are indeed blessed! I think that our teacher, our mother, Sarah Schenierer, is standing near us in this hour, listening to our talk and to the whisper of our hearts. And her holy soul is deriving pleasure from our readiness to die *al kiddush Hashem.* I see that her teachings have succeeded. The Bais Yaakov that she founded has brought forth such pure and holy daughters. Her spirit is hovering close. I feel her here with us, joining us and encouraging us in advance of the greatest and most holy *mitzvah* we will ever be called upon to perform."

A shiver went through the girls, and a great weeping burst from them.

The principal spoke again. "My dear daughters, I know that you are prepared for all sorts of suffering and torture. But those evil ones have something else in mind. Something much worse — something that has not even entered your minds. They want you to rebel against your Creator — to transgress His Will."

A silence hung in the room as the principal paused. She drew breath and continued, "The evil ones have decided to destroy our souls, not our bodies. They wish to defile us, Heaven forbid! They wish to keep our bodies alive so that they may contaminate our souls — Master of the Universe, make me strong! Help me do what I must do!"

Girls sobbed, girls cried out, others were silent, choked with emotion and fear.

The principal said, "Yes, my daughters. They want to steal what is most precious to us — our souls and bodies together. They want to force us to transgress our holy Torah."

Cries of despair burst from the girls. "What do we do? Who will help us?"

The principal soothed them. "Blessed is the One Who gives a man wisdom! There is a solution. Hashem, in His Goodness, has prepared a way out of this tragedy."

A questioning silence fell. The girls drank in every word the principal said next. "As we left our building, I took along pills of poison. They can save us from spiritual death, so that we may merit true life — eternal life."

Joyous cries sounded through the room. There was a sense of relief as the girls pressed forward, asking for the pills, each afraid that the supply would give out before her turn came. The principal pulled a small box from her purse, which she had managed to keep with her, and distributed the pills. Every girl guarded hers carefully, as though it were a precious ornament upon which her very life depended.

"Dear daughters," the principal said solemnly, "the time has come to perform this great *mitzvah*. Let us do it!" In a loud, clear voice, she recited the following prayer, which the girls repeated after her: *"Hineni muchenes umezumenes l'kayem mitzvas kiddush Hashem, l'shem yichud Kudshah brich Hu ushechintei al yedei hahu tamir v'ne'elam b'shem kol Yisrael"* — I am ready to fulfill the *mitzvah* of *kiddush Hashem*, for the sake of the unification of the Holy One, Blessed is He, and His Presence, through Him Who is hidden and inscrutable, (I pray) in the name of all Israel.

"Baruch atah Hashem Elokeinu Melech haolam, asher kidshanu bemitzvosav v'tzivanu al kiddush Hashem" — Blessed are You, O L-rd our G-d, King of the Universe, Who has sanctified us

with Your commandments and commanded us to sanctify Your Name.

Her voice grew stronger: *"Baruch atah Hashem Elokeinu Melech haolam, shehecheyanu v'kiyemanu v'higiyanu lazman hazeh"* — Blessed are You, O L-rd our G-d, King of the Universe, Who has kept us alive, sustained us, and brought us to this season!

In unison, they brought the pills to their lips and swallowed them. The pills contained a concentrated poison, powerful and terrible. A few minutes passed; the girls did not have much time to think about what was to come. The poison began to do its work.

I stood outside, watching, tears running down my cheeks. As the principal felt death steal upon her, she called out one last time, "My daughters, let us all say out loud together: *Shema Yisrael — Hashem Elokeinu — Hashem — Echad."*

The girls' voices rang out as one, loud and strong.

The effort spent the last of their strength. The voices were stilled — the voices of pure Jewish girls who had never tasted of sin in their short lives.

I burst into hysterical sobs. The soldier at the gate, having no idea of what was occurring inside, chased me away. I did not deserve a place among those pure and holy women and girls.

On the 13th day of Av, their souls rose to Heaven, accompanied by the spirits of their holy mothers. May those souls be linked to the chain of Life!

Chana Weiss

The following was written on behalf of the 93 teachers and students of the Bais Yaakov just hours before the Nazis came for them, and was sent to Rabbi Dr. Yitzchak Levine (son of Rabbi Aharon Levine, of Reisha) in New York.

✎ Last Testament of the 93

I do not know when this letter will reach you, or whether you will still remember me. We met at the conference in Marienbad. By the time you read this, I will no longer be counted among the living. In a few hours, all will belong to the past.

We had four rooms here. There are 93 of us, girls ranging from 14 to 22 years old, all students of Bais Yaakov. On the 27th of July, Gestapo agents rounded us up and threw us into a darkened room. We have only a little water to drink, and the girls are very frightened. But I comfort them with the thought that, in a little while, we will be together with our mother, Sarah.

Yesterday they removed us from the dark room and informed us that today the German soldiers will be coming to visit us, with the goal of having us transgress our holy faith. We immediately swore to die together. We have prepared poison. When the soldiers come, we will take it.

We have been here together all day, reciting the *viduy.* We are no longer afraid of anything. We have only one request: Say *Kaddish* for 93 Jewish girls who will soon be with Sarah, our mother.

(Signed) Chaya Feldman
Cracow

Part Three:
Pillars of Faith

🎗 Kaddish

A HIGHLY RESPECTED WOMAN, THE WIFE OF A prosperous businessman in the Hungarian city of Pressburg, adopted the custom of periodically donating a sum of money to the yeshivah, on the condition that someone there recite *Kaddish* for the souls of those unfortunates who have no one to say it for them. The yeshivah administration agreed, appointing one of the students to recite *Kaddish* for those departed souls.

After some time, the woman's husband passed away. His business suffered greatly without his leadership, and eventually fell into such dire straits that the woman was forced to close it down. Her financial situation worsened dramatically. As time passed, she was faced with a new problem. Her two daughters had reached marriageable age, but from where was the money to come for their dowries?

The mother bore her burdens in silence, courageously resigned to her fate. There was, however, one thing she was not willing to accept. The recitation of *Kaddish* must not stop just because she could no longer afford to pay her usual stipend. In great bitterness of spirit, she turned to the yeshivah administration, pleading with them to continue the *Kaddish* custom until her fortune turned and she would once again be able to pay.

The *Roshei Yeshivah*, moved by the widow's sincerity, agreed to do as she asked. The promise filled her with boundless joy. With beaming countenance, she left the yeshivah and started for home. Her situation did not press upon her quite as much as before. As long as *Kaddish* would be said, she felt she lacked nothing in this world. As far as her two daughters were concerned, she would place her trust in Hashem. The merciful Father of orphans and the compassionate Judge of widows would surely see their poverty and supply them with suitable bridegrooms and all their needs.

One day, as the woman stepped out into the street, she saw an elderly Jew approaching. His beard was full and white, and his face shone like the sun. The woman was startled by the warmth of his greeting — after all, the old man was a stranger to her. Her surprise grew when he began conversing with her, asking about her situation and that of her children.

The woman sighed deeply, pouring out the tale of her hardships. She described her fall from prosperity to poverty, to the point that she lacked the means with which to marry off her grown daughters.

"How much do you estimate you need for their wedding expenses?" the old man asked.

"What's the difference?" she sighed. "With all due respect, why do you wish to know?"

Rather than responding, however, the man pressed her for an answer until she gave him the estimate he wanted. Immediately, he drew a page from his notebook and wrote instructions to the local bank to pay her the amount she had mentioned.

Because this was a very large sum of money, he suggested to the stupefied widow, it was preferable that the note be signed in the presence of witnesses. They would see with their own eyes that he was signing over the money, and would add their own signatures to that effect.

Astonished and shaken, the widow went to the yeshivah to request that two students accompany her. The old man asked them to witness his signature on the check. For additional security, he asked them for a piece of paper, on which he signed his name once again for authentication purposes. He handed the check to the woman with instructions to redeem it at the bank on the following morning.

The whole business seemed extraordinary to her. Why had the old man, a stranger to her, seen fit to show her such largess — to the point of covering the entire wedding expenses for her two daughters? Nevertheless, she hurried to the bank the next day to try her luck.

When the bank clerk read the check, he stared at the widow in amazement. He looked at the check again, then again at the widow. In some confusion, he asked her to wait. Check in hand, he went into the manager's office.

The bank manager took one look at the check — and fainted dead away!

A babble of distress and bewilderment arose from every corner of the bank. The clerks, hearing of the incident, hustled the widow into a small room and stood guard over her to make certain she did not leave. Clearly, something was amiss.

When the manager recovered consciousness, he demanded to see the woman who had brought in the check. As she stood before him, trembling, he demanded an accounting of how she had come by the check.

"I received it just yesterday from a very respectable Jew. There were two witnesses to his signature, too," she explained anxiously.

"Would you be able to identify the man who gave you the check, if you saw a picture of him?" the manager asked.

"Of course I could! And I have no doubt that the two yeshivah students who witnessed his signature could identify him as well."

The manager reached into his desk and pulled out a picture.

"Yes!" The woman beamed. "That's the man. He's the one who so generously gave me the check."

Slowly, the manager turned to his clerks. "Give this woman the money," he ordered. "And then let her go."

It was only after the widow's departure that he confided his story to those present, who were naturally agog with curiosity.

"The man who gave that woman the check," he said, "was my father — who passed away 10 years ago. Last night, he appeared in a dream and told me these words: 'Know this. Since you strayed from the true path and married a Gentile woman and stopped reciting *Kaddish* for me, my soul found no rest — until this woman, this widow, came and arranged for the recitation of *Kaddish* for those who have no one to say it for them. The *Kaddish* they said for me in the yeshivah, on that woman's instructions, led to ascendancy and peace for my soul.'

"'Tomorrow morning, this woman will appear in your bank with a check that I have given her to cover her daughters' wedding expenses.'

"When I woke up this morning, I was shaken by the dream. I described it to my wife, who just laughed. But when the woman appeared with the check, I realized that the dream had come true."

Reb Chaim Sonnenfeld would tell this story, always ending with, "And who were the two yeshivah boys who witnessed the signature? I was one, and the other was my friend, Reb Yehudah Greenwald."

The bank manager's life was never the same. He repented and found his way back into the fold of *Klal Yisrael*. His wife became a sincere convert to Judaism, and together the two of them knew the joy of building a fine Jewish home.

❦ "Shema Yisrael" in Treblinka

The renowned author Rachel Auerbach relates the following story:

A young boy who escaped from Treblinka told me of something he had witnessed in the hut where prisoners were prepared for the gas chambers. This particular group was comprised of many women and children. One woman stood out, taller than the rest, and wearing an unusual headdress. She stood in a corner, face to the wall — the "east wall" of her imagination. Behind her stood other women, facing the same depraved wall in that chamber of death.

Like a cantor on Yom Kippur — or spokesperson for the doomed — the woman stood and prayed there in Treblinka, on the brink of extinction. In Yiddish words, chanted to the High Holy Days melodies, the words burst from her heart:

"*Shema Yisrael, Hashem Elokeinu, Hashem Echad!*" she cried. "Master of the Universe, You are the One and Only. We have no other Father besides You. Open Your eyes and see our suffering. See our humiliation and hear our children's cries! Remove sin from us so that we may merit — like our fathers, Avraham, Yitzchak and Yaakov, and our mothers, Sarah, Rivkah, Rachel and Leah — to be with them, with all our loved ones — Most merciful One in Heaven!"

She spread her hands skyward, as the women grouped behind her moved pale lips, word for word, in an echo of her prayer. As if reciting the blessing over the Shabbos candles, they covered their faces with their hands, tears trickling through their fingers.

A single sob burst from the tall woman's throat, and then she fell silent. Behind her, the death hut shook with the other women's wails, turning the room into a place reminiscent of an *Ezras Nashim* on Yom Kippur.

❧ "And Thou Shalt Love …"

When Reb Avraham, the Chofetz Chaim's son, passed away, the Chofetz Chaim stood silently at his bedside. Presently, he told a story brought down in the book *Toldos Adam*:

"During the Spanish Inquisition, in the year 5252 (1492), a Jewish woman watched the bloodthirsty evildoers slaughter her two beloved children. The good woman, brokenhearted, raised her eyes to Heaven and whispered, 'Master of the Universe! I have always loved You — but as long as I had my beloved children my heart was divided in two. But now — now that my children are no longer here, my heart has become filled with nothing but a burning love for You. Now I can truly fulfill the *mitzvah* of *V'ahavta es Hashem Elokecha b'chol levovcha u'vchol nafshecha* — And you shall love Hashem, your G-d, with all your heart and with all your soul."

As the Chofetz Chaim finished the story, he paused, then proclaimed in a loud and energetic voice, "Master of the Universe, the love I have given until now to my son, I give to You!"

❧ A Mother of Old

The evil regime ordered the Jewish youths of the town gathered up and incarcerated in the local shul. By decree, they were to renounce their faith — or die.

Hundreds of townspeople gathered outside the shul, praying with all their might, and beseeching the Almighty to spare the boys. Women sobbed with a fervor that tore at the heart, and fathers shouted their pleas from the depths of their being. The entire town was paralyzed.

Inside the shul, the young men stood steadfast and stubborn. They would not renounce their faith, they declared, even on pain of death. Furious, the Christians drew their swords and beheaded them. The heads were placed in a large sack and tossed into the crowd outside.

As soon as the sack was opened, the tragedy became known. Heartrending cries rose on every side. Women and men, seeing the proof of their sons' end, wailed in horrific pain. In the midst of this scene of awful anguish, a woman shoved her way through the crowd. She was the mother of one of the youths in the shul. Approaching the sack, she demanded to know if her son had been among those killed. The moment she caught sight of her son's head, she broke into a joyous dance!

It seemed as though she had lost her mind. Every eye stared at her in shock, but the woman danced on, praise for Hashem pouring out of her with every step. At last, she was asked for the meaning of this strange behavior.

"You were crying for fear your sons would be killed," she explained. "*I* wept for fear my son would renounce his faith! Now that I see that he stood up to the test, how can I not rejoice?"

❧ The Overdue Letter

Rabbi Yitzchak Weinstein, *mechutan* of the Brisker Rebbe, lost his father while still a child. In time, his mother remarried a man whose name, as it happened, was also Reb Yitzchak. Young Yitzchak, an only child, was sent off to learn in a large yeshivah, several days' journey from his mother's home. In later years he would tell a remarkable story connected with that period of his life — a story that highlights his mother's extraordinary faith.

Fear and trepidation reigned throughout Russia. Cells of revolutionaries operated in different parts of the country, determined to topple the cruel Czar. Naturally, the Czar's men strove forcefully to suppress these efforts. In their pursuit of Communist revolutionaries, the Czar's loyalists knew no mercy. The sound of gunfire became commonplace in Russia, along with acts of murder and mayhem.

To conceal their activities from the authorities, the revolutionaries often sought out shuls and *batei midrash*. The Communists would burst in without warning, taking over the place for their own use, conducting meetings and organizing their affairs. No one dared protest. The Communists held the populace in a grip of terror, threatening dire retaliation against anyone who might compromise them to the government.

It goes without saying that these activities exposed the local citizenry to myriad dangers. In due course the police learned of this stratagem, and often men who had been peacefully *davening* or learning were forced to flee for their lives at the first sign of the Czar's officers. Sadly, there was an additional danger: A good many young Jews were caught up in the revolutionary fervor, and joined the Communists in their visionary but godless dreams.

One day, young Yitzchak's mother learned that Communists had called a meeting in her son's yeshivah building, and that the authorities, hearing of this, had sent in the police. In the ensuing gunfire, one of the yeshivah students attending the meeting had been killed.

Anxiously, the mother awaited word of her son. Weeks passed without a letter from him. The silence frightened and grieved her. She was certain that she had lost her only child.

On his return from shul every morning, her husband, Reb Yitzchak, would ask if there was any news of her son. Soon he had no need to ask, for the answer was written plainly in the deepening lines on her face, and her worried sighs. And still there was no word of young Yitzchak.

One morning, however, Reb Yitzchak returned home to find his wife's face wreathed in smiles. He rejoiced, expecting to hear that she had received a letter or some other indication that her son was alive. Imagine his surprise, when — in response to his inquiry — she informed him that there had been no letter.

"In that case, why do you look so happy?" he asked, bewildered.

She replied, "After thinking about it deeply, I've reached the conclusion that there's no reason to be upset. And shall I tell you why? If my son has become a Communist, I have no need to mourn his death!"

Thus the power of a Jewish mother and her pure and holy faith in all its simplicity.

🐞 A Trusting Heart

The wife of Reb Aryeh Levine, the *tzaddik* of Jerusalem, was a paragon of belief in Hashem. He would say of her, "My wife reached such a high level, that if something was decreed upon her from Heaven there was no need for her to accept it with love. She simply did not feel any pain, disappointment, or anguish." This, he said, was a higher level than that of turning negative feelings into acceptance.

He would also say that any good *middos* he had were his only by virtue of the strength of his wife's faith. She never complained or worried about the future. Her trust in Heaven simply knew no limit. "Without her," he would say, "it would have been impossible for me to withstand the famine of World War One. Her *bitachon* in *HaKadosh Baruch Hu* was greater than mine."

It was a terrible famine. The crisis reached a crescendo, and Reb Aryeh did not know where to turn. His children were crying, not having eaten for two days.

Reb Aryeh heard of a man in Jerusalem who lent money to the needy of his city. Having done a favor for this man in the past, Reb Aryeh yielded to his wife's request and went to the man's house, taking with him several valuable manuscripts from his own library. He asked for a loan, offering to leave the books behind as collateral.

To his shock, the man refused to lend him the money. Reb Aryeh asked, "On what do you base your refusal, when you've been lending money to other people?"

The man replied, "I have to lend to the others, because they know that I'm rich and would harbor a grudge against me if I refused them the money they want. But I know that you won't bear me a grudge even if I refuse you."

Deeply disappointed, Reb Aryeh returned home. He went into his room and broke into bitter tears. "Because I won't hold a grudge, I'm to be refused a loan and be forced to succumb to famine?"

His wife began to encourage and comfort him. "Reb Aryeh, Reb Aryeh, where is your Yiddishkeit? Where is your trust in *HaKadosh Baruch Hu*? Just think for a minute why that man refused you the loan.

"Was it because he doesn't have the money? He's a rich man! Is it because he's not accustomed to lending out money? But we know that he's made many loans to the needy. Is it because he doesn't trust you to pay it back? Just last month, you knocked on his door in the middle of the night to return a gold coin that he left in our house when he changed money for you. He knows that you're honest. Why, then, won't he lend you money?"

The Rebbetzin paused, then concluded, "We must judge every person favorably — but what do we do when we simply can't find any excuse for someone? Let us say, then, that something out of the ordinary is happening. Heaven is preventing that man from lending you money, so that your salvation may come from another source. Reb Aryeh, throw your burden on Hashem, and He will support you!"

Reb Aryeh was calmed by his wife's words, and stopped weeping. He understood that she was right, and that he must strengthen his own trust.

Later that same day, there came a knock on the Levines' door. It was the mailman, bearing a letter from America. Opening the envelope, Reb Aryeh found a letter and a check for $10 — a very respectable sum at that time!

The letter was from an American Jew whom Reb Aryeh had met several years earlier, in Petach Tikvah. The American had asked Reb Aryeh whether he was the grandson of so-and-so.

Upon Reb Aryeh responding in the affirmative, the American said, "You resemble your dear departed grandfather, whom I greatly respected." The two men had parted amicably, and had never met again.

The American subsequently passed on, and in his will ordered a check for $10 to be sent to Reb Aryeh Levine on the anniversary of his passing.

Reb Aryeh's wife was right: The salvation had come from another source.

Part Four:

Person to Person

❧ A Grudging Heart

RABBI SHIMSHON, THE *RAV* OF ZIVLIN, POSSESSED extraordinary modesty and humility. He lived and worked among his people until, on the third day of Elul 5507 (1747) he was summoned back to his Maker. This *tzaddik* was a hidden light, and the greater part of his accomplishments was never made known to the public. The few things we do know about Reb Shimshon earn him a place in the annals of our nation's great men.

The *Bircas Avraham* was fond of repeating the following story:

When Rabbi Shimson became the rabbi of Zivlin, he made the following stipulations to the community leaders: Every major decision concerning the community must be brought to him — but only on *Motza'ei Shabbos*. His habit was to learn in the *beis midrash* from Sunday through Friday, answering halachic questions during that time. On *Erev Shabbos* he would return home.

One weekday, the Rabbi's wife went to the marketplace to purchase food for the family. Her eye fell upon a large and splendid fish — perfect for Shabbos. Unfortunately, the wife of the richest man in town noticed the fish at the same moment, and claimed it for her own. The vendor took advantage of the situation to raise the price. The two women exchanged words, in the course of which the rich woman seriously insulted the Rabbi's wife.

The honor of the Torah had been impugned! The story spread through the town. It reached the ears of the community leaders, who determined that the woman must be punished. Though her husband was rich and powerful, the insult to the Torah must be avenged!

This matter, the leaders reluctantly agreed, was serious enough to warrant the Rabbi's attention. According to the conditions laid down when he undertook the position, they could not make a move until they had consulted with him, and this was impossible until the following *Motza'ei Shabbos*. Meanwhile, they visited the Rebbetzin, asking her to use her own wisdom to present the situation to her husband, over Shabbos, in such a way that he would be favorably disposed toward their position come *Motza'ei Shabbos*.

On Friday night, when Reb Shimshon returned home from shul, he was met with a surprise. Instead of sitting beside the set dining room table, as was her custom, the Rebbetzin was seated in a corner of the room, by a different, much smaller table.

"What do I see here?" he asked in wonder.

She replied, "It's because I don't deserve to be a Rebbetzin, or to sit at the Rav's table. That's why I've prepared a separate table for myself."

Wonder had turned to shock. "Why don't you deserve to be the Rebbetzin?"

"Because the rich man's wife called me ..." And she told him the whole story.

"She insulted you in that way, and people are silent? Where is respect for the Torah? What did the community leaders have to say?"

She answered, "The entire community was shaken up by the incident. The community leaders decided to fine the woman — but their hands are tied, because you insist that they do nothing without consulting you, and they can't ask you until *Motza'ei Shabbos!*"

The Rabbi fell silent. He began preparing for the Shabbos meal, persuading his wife to rejoin him at the table. As he stood up to recite *Kiddush*, a brimming cup of wine in his hand, a sudden thought occurred to him.

"When did the incident take place?"

"This past Tuesday."

"Tuesday? Tuesday?" The rabbi was appalled. "And from Tuesday until today you have been harboring a grudge against a Jewish woman? You have not yet forgiven her?"

The Rebbetzin was thrown into confusion. Her righteous husband's words pierced her heart. Immediately, she said, "I forgive her!"

The Rabbi told his wife, "That's not enough. For a Jew to harbor a grudge in his heart from Tuesday to Shabbos, there must be some sort of personal apology. Let's go."

The Rebbetzin was taken aback. Wasn't it enough that the rich woman had insulted her, causing her public embarrassment and humiliation? Must she actually go over to that person's house and beg forgiveness for harboring a grudge? However, she deeply honored her husband and his teachings. The two donned their coats and went out into the dark, leaving the cup of wine untouched on the table.

They reached the rich man's house and knocked on the door.

"Who's there?" a voice called.

The Rabbi identified himself by name. Rightly suspecting that this unexpected visit concerned the previous Tuesday's episode in the marketplace, the household was thrown into a panic. They held the Rabbi in awe, and dreaded his wrath. Opening the door, they fell at his feet, weeping and pleading for his forgiveness.

The Rabbi stopped them. "Do you have to ask us for forgiveness, when we have come to ask the same thing of you — for the grudge my wife has held against the woman of your house since Tuesday?"

Shock overwhelmed the family. They cried, "Do you have to ask *us* for forgiveness? It was our home that produced this insult to the Torah. We are the ones who have sinned, not you!"

Both sides shed tears, each offering apologies to the other, until their voices mingled in cries of, "You are forgiven!" and their hearts united in friendship.

Only then was Reb Shimshon satisfied. And only then did he and the Rebbetzin return to their own home, to recite *Kiddush* on the wine and usher in a Shabbos of peace and joy.

❧ A Woman of Tact

A prominent Orthodox journalist recounted the following incident:

In the year 5691 (1931), I visited Sarah Schenierer's home on the occasion of her father's *yahrtzeit*. I found her seated at the table — learning a *perek* of *mishnayos*.

Looking up, she greeted me and said, "It's a good thing you came. Before you tell me why you're here, I'd like to ask for your help in explaining this *mishnah* to me. I'm finding it unclear."

As I expounded on the *mishnah*, her eyes lit up. Satisfied, she sat back and inquired about the reason for my visit.

To my amazement and embarrassment, I could not recall

why I had come. The reason had simply escaped my mind! I sat there, silent and ashamed, straining to remember. Sarah Schenierer discerned my distress at once. In an effort to relieve my embarrassment, she said, "You know what it is? You were sent here by Heaven to explain this *mishnah* to me!"

Then, to distract me, she began to share some of the thoughts she'd heard from various Torah scholars about the significance of a *yahrtzeit*. "In general, I don't like the noise and tumult that people make at every opportunity for festivity. But one thing I do like, and very much, is to try whenever possible to commemorate the *yahrtzeit* of relatives and *tzaddikim*. It serves a very good purpose, helping both the dead and the living. Today happens to be the *yahrtzeit* of my father. It's a day that influences me more than any other in my life."

I exhaled with relief, confused no longer.

✎ Brief Meeting

Sarah Schenierer was traveling by train, en route to a Bais Yaakov convention. At a certain station along the way, the entire student body of the local Bais Yaakov and their teacher turned out to greet her through the train window. As the train pulled into the station, Sarah Schenierer heard girls' voices calling her name. She hurried to the window, but by the time she got there the train had started moving again.

The girls' disappointment was boundless. Many had tears in their eyes. Sarah Schenierer had no choice but to wave to them from the rapidly departing train.

As soon as she arrived at her destination, she sat down and penned the following letter to those students:

"Dear girls, may your lives be long and good! I saw you, I heard you, only for a moment. But do not let that fact distress you. *Ki rega b'apo* — your anger that our meeting lasted no longer than a minute — *chayim bi'retzono* — my will and my aspirations are with you all of our lives!"

This heartfelt letter reached the girls, transforming anger and disappointment into happiness and peace of mind.

❧ Not Even a Trace

The quiet city of Lucerne, nestled at the foot of the Swiss Alps, was a place where the Jewish community could exist in peace and security. A number of wonderful families thrived there, among them that of Rabbi Shimshon Raphael Erlanger, a man who radiated love of his fellow Jew. His door was always open; his home was a gathering-place for Torah scholars and a source of warmth and lovingkindness for all.

His good wife, Tova, was a noble soul. So righteous was she that there were those who credited her with having *ruach hakodesh*. Tova's exalted notions and the atmosphere she created around her underscored the Divine Presence within her home. Hers was the spirit that made the house a G-dly one, whether in preparing a magnificent table to honor the Shabbos, or supervising the decoration of the *succah,* or in guiding and encouraging her sons in their Torah study.

There were 11 beautiful flowers in Tova's bouquet: 11 children of whom any mother might be proud. Into each she breathed her loving ambition for their excellence in Torah and *mitzvos.*

Sadly, Tova was not granted a long life. Before her death, her eminence and Divine spirit became abundantly clear. She was able to predict to her husband, weeks beforehand, the exact date when a eulogy would be printed in the newspaper.

It was Succos when her illness took a grave turn. With

amazing reserves of strength, she asked her husband for *hoshanos* and recited the appropriate *tefillos*. Then she handed the *aravos* back to her husband, saying, "Please place these in my grave with me. This is my last *mitzvah* in the world of doing."

The hour of her passing drew near. The house was wrapped in a brooding anxiety. On Simchas Torah, Tova's husband sat beside her, watching over his sick wife and praying for her recovery — while Tova herself offered words of encouragement and comfort.

Everywhere, Jews were busy dancing in honor of the Torah. This woman, whose love for the Torah surpassed any other feeling, urged her husband to go to shul to dance and rejoice … yes, to rejoice with the Torah, even in such a difficult time. Nothing, Tova maintained, should mar the joy of Simchas Torah. It would comfort her and give her peace of mind to see him do as she asked.

By the next day, her condition had deteriorated rapidly. Death was clearly very near. Her husband asked, "Are you afraid of dying?"

Tova answered bravely, "Have these ears ever listened to *lashon hara*? Have these lips every spoken *lashon hara*? Why, then, should I be afraid of death?"

Two days after Simchas Torah, Tova passed away at the age of 41. She left behind her respected husband and 11 children, all of whom spent the rest of their lives dedicated to the Torah and merited establishing fine and honorable Jewish homes.

On her tombstone, the following words are engraved: "She despised even the trace of *lashon hara*."

❧ One Woman's Mission

Mrs. Chedvah Zilberfarb's name has become synonymous with *shemiras halashon*. Through her tireless efforts — and, even more, through personal example — she taught many, many people the value of guarding their speech.

When still a student at Bais Yaakov High School, she established a weekly study session with her friends on the Chofetz Chaim's *Shemiras HaLashon*. The number of girls who participated in this worthwhile activity varied. At times — especially at first — the number was very small. Sometimes, Chedvah was mocked by some of the more lighthearted girls. But she continued undaunted. She knew how great a reward lay in store for those who guard their tongues, and what dangers lurk in wait for those who fail. Facing down the mockers, she persisted in her modest way at any cost.

The more she studied the laws pertaining to proper speech, the more she understood how necessary it is to refrain from speech which is improper. Gradually, she transformed herself into a model of circumspection in this important area.

Later in her life, she began to courageously spread the idea further afield, giving lectures on the topic and gathering around her a nucleus of serious-minded women who drank in her words. Even when diagnosed with a mortal illness, she never stopped. Chedvah succeeded in turning a dread disease into a spiritual force for self-elevation and community improvement. Rather than lock herself away with her personal pain, she translated that pain into an urgent spiritual message. She became a shofar, trumpeting out her message for all who would listen: "Please, stop your tongues from speaking evil!"

From school to school, from program to program, from lecture to lecture, she hurried to raise community consciousness in this vital area. Though breathing with difficulty and weak of limb, she nevertheless coped with an exhausting schedule of appearances in Israel, the United States and Europe, where thousands flocked to her banner, forming groups of their own to strengthen *shemiras halashon* in their own communities.

She found a way into every heart — of adults and children alike, women from Israel and from the Diaspora — women of every stripe. Her message addressed each on her own level, each according to her own aspirations.

On the 13th day of Kislev 5750 (1990), Chedvah left this world. Thousands attended her funeral, weeping for the pure tongue now consigned to the earth. There is no calculating the impact of this one woman in spreading the crucial tenets of *shemiras halashon* — an impact that still reverberates to this day.

❧ A Time to Bow

Among the many sterling qualities of Rebbetzin Chaya Rivka Shinalson (d. 5755 [1995]) was an extreme caution in how she used her words. She was always very wary of saying anything that might border on *lashon hara*, and was especially careful never to insult or belittle another person — even if that person was trying to belittle her. "Better to appear stupid and not answer," she would often say, "than to answer back and be considered an evildoer by Heaven."

As she taught her children and all those who spent time in her home, there is a valuable lesson to be learned from the last part of the *Amidah*, where we say the words *Oseh shalom*: Sometimes, for the sake of peace, one must bow and step back.

❧ Impeccable Logic

A rich man wanted to help a Torah scholar who was blessed with a large family. His plan was to buy the scholar a larger apartment. However, he knew that broaching the subject directly would be of no use: The scholar would reject the offer. Instead, the rich man approached the scholar's mother, herself a woman well known for her righteousness. He hoped that she would persuade her son to accept his offer of a larger apartment.

In his meeting with the mother, the rich man presented many cogent reasons for the son to make the move. He would have peace of mind for his Torah study; his family would live more contentedly in the larger space; his children would flourish in the new conditions. If it was possible to achieve all this without running into debt, why not do it?

The mother answered, "Whether or not your arguments are sound is beside the point. What is clear, however, is that my son is not the only one living under difficult conditions. There are many other families of *bnei Torah* who don't have a penny to spare and who have no opportunity to move to new apartments. If my son accepts your offer and moves, the same ambition will automatically enter the hearts of all the other men in his position. One of them may go into debt, all because of my son. I am not prepared to see that happen."

And so, the family of 13 continued to live in a two-room apartment.

~ Fair Wages

The wife of Reb Zusha of Hanipole gave a beautiful piece of cloth to a tailor so that he might sew her a dress. When the tailor completed his work he carried it to the Rebbetzin's house. Setting it down, he sighed deeply.

"What's the matter?" the Rebbetzin asked. "Why do you sigh like that?"

In great pain, he replied, "My daughter has become engaged to a fine young man. One day, seeing me sewing a woman's dress, he thought that it was for his bride. Learning that it would not be hers has filled him with anguish."

The Rebbetzin's compassion overwhelmed her. She picked up the dress and handed it to the tailor. "This is a present for your daughter, the *kallah*," she said.

Later, relating the tale to her husband, Reb Zusha immediately asked her, "Have you paid the tailor?"

"What do you mean?" she asked in surprise. "I gave him the whole dress as a present! What's there to pay for?"

Reb Zusha answered, "That poor tailor labored a full week for *you*, and not for his daughter. With tired eyes, longing to be finished, he worked on and on so that he might earn a little money for his family. Now what will he eat? Just because you were good enough to give him a present for his daughter, does that mean that he should be cheated out of his due wages?"

The Rebbetzin wasted no time. She left the house at once, to go pay the tailor.

❧ Every Penny Counts

Rebbetzin Fraidel Chaikin was scrupulous with the funds of her husband's yeshivah at Aix-la-Bains, France. As *Rosh Yeshivah*, Rabbi Chaim Chaikin and his family lived in the yeshivah and received full board at its expense. The family's daily fare came from the yeshivah's kitchens.

In the Rebbetzin's opinion, every penny she spent was at the expense of a page of Gemara that could have been learned. When she selected vegetables from the yeshivah's stores, she was always careful to pick the damaged ones. Day-old bread was all she would take for her family, because the yeshivah boys did not like to eat it.

Even when it came to using tap water, the Rebbetzin reminded her household not to be wasteful. "The yeshivah's water," she would say, "is worth gold!"

The Chofetz Chaim's sister had a similar sense of responsibility when it came to other people's money. There was a period of time when she rarely left her home. Not even on the High Holy Days did she venture out to shul. Finally, the Chofetz Chaim asked for an explanation.

Surprised, she replied, "What, are you also asking me that question? The answer is obvious! It's well known that I keep money in my house that has been collected for widows and orphans. How can I leave the house? I have a responsibility to make sure that money is safe!"

Part Five:

A Heavenly Attitude

🍂 Reserves of Strength

RABBI YOSEF NECHEMIAH KORNITZER SERVED AS RAV of Cracow for many years. To the shock of the entire community, he passed away suddenly in 5693 (1933), immediately after his son, Shimon, became engaged. The sense of grief and bereavement cast a black shadow over the joy of the occasion, until it was impossible to separate one emotion from the other. No one could believe that Reb Yosef Nechemiah would not be present to share in his son's simchah. It was up to the widow, Breindel — daughter of Rav Pinchas Chaim Klein, Rav of Selish — to marry off her son.

The wedding had been set for a date after Shavuos, just a month and a half after Reb Yosef Nechemiah's passing. Despite the universal mourning, it was deemed proper to go ahead with the plans as originally scheduled. The family prepared to travel from Cracow to the town where the wedding was to be held.

A great number of people came to see them off at the train station. The void left by the death of the Rav was very much on the minds of every one present, and the atmosphere at the station was funereal. Tears clouded many eyes. As soon as the train pulled away, the crowd gave way to its grief and wept copiously.

At that same moment, Rebbetzin Breindel, the widowed mother of the *chasan*, turned to her grieving family. With extraordinary strength of character, she said, "My children — stop, please. Don't cry now. We are on our way to celebrate Reb Shimon's marriage."

Thus spoke the bereft wife who knew how to rise above her pain in order to fulfill the will of her Father above.

Another story is told of the remarkable self-discipline that Rebbetzin Breindel of Cracow was able to summon at need.

In the year 5681 (1921), her firstborn son, Akiva, passed away at the age of 18. Upon hearing the news, Breindel was inconsolable. For long hours she wept incessantly.

Then her father, the Selisher Rav, walked into the room. Instantly, the tears stopped. Out of respect for her father she pulled herself to her feet. Then she walked over to him, kissed his hand and offered him a seat. Every trace of her bitter weeping had vanished without a trace.

Breindel was able to master her own emotions for the higher purpose of sparing her father additional pain. To minimize her father's distress, the grieving mother succeeded in summoning up reserves of hidden strength that stand as an example and an ideal for us all.

🍃 An Unusual Request

The Chasam Sofer's great-grandson wrote the following about his grandmother, daughter of that great *tzaddik:*

My father related to me that my grandmother, Gittel, was a very beautiful woman, with a face that shone like the sun. In her great modesty, she hid herself as much as possible from the public, and never went out into the marketplace except in times of true necessity.

On one such occasion, despite all her precautions, a man caught sight of Gittel and followed her, wanting to gaze at her. Enormously distressed, she hurried home and took up the *Tehillim* that her father, the Chasam Sofer, used in times of trouble. With tears running down her cheeks, she beseeched Hashem to take away her beauty.

The Chasam Sofer, returning home to the sight of his daughter sitting in a corner and praying with a tearstained face, was alarmed. "My daughter," he said, "why are you crying so bitterly? What is troubling you?"

She answered, "I know that people say I'm beautiful, and that frivolous men in the street might see me and become ensnared in sin. It happened that way just now, as I walked in the marketplace. I've been *davening* about this, and crying. It pains me to know that I may be a stumbling block for people! I was pleading with Hashem to remove my beauty, so that no wrong shall be done because of me."

Hearing this, her father was deeply moved. "Hashem has blessed you, my daughter. You have spoken the truth. And because your intentions are *l'shem Shamayim*, I will add my own prayers to yours. May Hashem grant your wish. You are expecting a baby, and because you are willing to give up your physical radiance, you will merit giving birth to a son who will light up the Jewish people with his Torah."

Sure enough, a short time later Gittel became ill. When the sickness passed, she was restored to her former strength and health — but her face had changed. The radiance was gone, along with the special glow. And soon afterward, she gave birth to the Cheishev Sofer, who was an outstanding figure of piety and Torah, just as his grandfather, the holy Chasam Sofer, had predicted.

ঌ Let the Walls Bear Witness

When the righteous woman, Mrs. Ruth Kaplan, passed away at the young age of 28, her husband requested that the funeral procession go past their house, so that he might eulogize her near the walls of the home that they had shared.

As Ruth was brought to her final resting place, the mood among those accompanying her was one of anguish. She had been a very young woman when she died, leaving behind tender orphans and a grieving husband. Standing on the doorstep of their house, her husband, the prestigious Rabbi Tzvi Kaplan, said, "I have brought my wife here, near our house, in order to arouse Heaven in the merit of her righteous ways. Master of the Universe, You know that from the moment we married, the walls of our home never saw the hairs of her head!"

Who is better equipped to testify to a woman's piety than her own husband?

It is said of the Chazon Ish's mother that when asked in what merit she had been blessed with sons and sons-in-law who were such giants in Torah, she replied, "The walls of my house never saw a hair of my head." Even when she washed her hair on *Erev Shabbos,* two women would stand beside her, holding out sheets to block every strand of her hair from the walls' view.

✖ The London Rebbetzin

Rabbi Yechezkel Abramsky was appointed Chief Rabbi of London. As a matter of course, his wife accompanied him to various official functions. She did not buy many clothes, preferring to wear one dress for several years, only changing some accessory from time to time. When asked why she did not indulge herself with new clothing, her answer was clear: "For the price of a new dress, you can print nearly an additional volume of your *Chazon Yechezkel.*"

The only time the Rebbetzin was honored at a public appearance in her own right was at the inauguration of a religious school in Manchester. The Rebbetzin was asked to cut the ribbon, to symbolize the school's opening. In accordance with the English custom, she was presented with a gold key as a souvenir of the occasion.

Later, after the Abramskys had moved to *Eretz Yisrael,* a certain *Rosh Yeshivah* visited their home, anxiety clearly stamped on his features. It seemed that his yeshivah's chief supporter had passed away, and the widow had sent a telegram announcing her intended presence at the yeshivah's upcoming *chanukas habayis.* How, he was wondering now, should he appropriately honor her visit?

As he and Rabbi Abramski sat pondering the question, the

Rebbetzin entered the room — her own gold key in hand. The *Rosh Yeshivah's* daughter, she suggested, should give the widow the key in the course of the ceremony.

Two weeks later, the *Rosh Yeshivah* visited the Abramskys again. He showed them a photograph the widow had sent him, in which she wore the gold key sewn onto her dress in the form of a brooch. Along with the picture she had sent a generous check.

One year, the Rabbi and his Rebbetzin flew back to London to visit their son. During the trip the Rebbetzin felt weak, but hid the fact from her husband. Upon their arrival in London, however, the weakness grew more pronounced, and she had to be hospitalized.

The doctors there made a faulty diagnosis. At one point, thinking her asleep, they stood by the Rebbetzin's bed talking to each other. She heard them say that she had just weeks to live.

She did not panic. She evinced no depression or hysteria. Instead, she wrote a letter to her grandson on the occasion of his sixth birthday, exhorting him to learn Torah so that he might carry on the family's golden tradition.

A few days later the Rebbetzin recovered, and was able to return together with her husband to their home in *Eretz Yisrael*.

About two weeks before her death, the Rebbetzin summoned her daughter-in-law and asked her to take a certain jacket of her husband's to the cleaner's. That jacket, she said, was the one he would wear to fulfill the mitzvah of *keriah* (the tearing of a mourner's clothes) and of sitting *shivah* (the seven days of mourning). It would not be proper for him to sit in a jacket that was not clean.

❧ A Long-Deferred Joy

The Kaliver Rebbe enjoyed relating this moving story that he had heard from a Jew who lived in the Soviet Union during the difficult Iron Curtain era.

The Jew was one of a secret group of men who attended the *bris milah* of newborn Jewish babies. This was an activity attended with grave risk. Anyone caught circumcising his son was immediately harassed by the authorities. The persecution could range from having the father fired from his job to having him sent into exile in some remote region of the Soviet Union. Those who participated in any way in the illegal ceremony were subject to the same dangers. A *minyan* of loyal and dependable Jews, therefore, was chosen to attend each *bris* and to keep it secret.

On one occasion, a senior army officer came surreptitiously to this *minyan* to invite them to a *bris* to be held on the following day. They arrived at the appointed place, and found the officer awaiting them. He led them to a house situated in an inner courtyard. The tables were set with delicacies and the place wore an air of joyous festivity, as though they were not in the heart of the Soviet Union at all. A short time later, the baby was brought in, and the *bris milah* was performed. Then — just seconds after the baby was returned to his mother — a sudden outcry arose. The mother had fainted!

Everyone rushed into the room to see what had happened. Eventually, the mother regained consciousness. Asked for an explanation, she provided one that sent shivers down every back.

"My baby," she said, "is over a year old. My husband and I have been waiting impatiently all these months for a chance to give him a *bris* in safety. And for this entire year, I have not let myself kiss my son. Each time I was about to kiss him, I would think: How can I kiss a baby who has not been circumcised?

"Just now, when they brought the baby to me after the *bris*, I gave him his first kiss. My emotion overpowered me — and I fainted!"

❧ A Mother's Plea

During the infamous reign of the Nazis, when children were wrested from their parents' arms and fathers taken from their families, Rabbi Yisrael Spira, the Bluzhever Rebbe, was transported to a labor camp. His job was sawing wood.

As he worked, his heart was filled with Hashem's Presence. He pushed and pulled at the saw, splitting tree trunks in a steady progression. The German soldier supervising him made sure — by careful scrutiny and periodic hurled abuse — that the Rebbe never paused in his labor. Undaunted, the Bluzhever's face shone with a warmth that affected all who were near.

The squeal of brakes sounded near the camp gates. At a barked order, a group of women descended, pale and spent to the point of utter exhaustion. Suddenly, one of the women veered sharply in the Bluzhever's direction, coming straight at him with wild, hunted eyes. Setting down her bundle, she cried, "A knife, Rebbe! Give me a knife right away!"

The Bluzhever continued sawing. His face remained impassive, his hands in constant motion. One wrong word could cost a life.

The woman sent a beseeching look at the Rebbe, and begged again, "A knife, Rebbe!"

"It is forbidden," the Rebbe answered softly, still plying the saw. "A Jewish daughter is not permitted to take her own life. It is absolutely forbidden! The Creator that makes the furnace burn can also put it out — and He can also not put it out — The flames will lick our bodies at His Will, and we will be summoned as pure sacrifices —"

A heavy hand came down on his neck. The Kapo loved trivial crimes, like this whispering. He stormed at the Rebbe, "You were talking, you Jew dog! I saw you talking! You committed a crime! You will stop at once!"

The Rebbe spoke calmly and pleasantly as he responded to the Kapo. "The woman," he explained, "asked me for a knife. The request of a knife is no crime, and she did not communicate further with me."

The Kapo smirked. Here was a chance for some fun! Drawing his own knife from his belt, he handed it to the woman.

Her face lit up. She snatched the knife eagerly, as though afraid he would change his mind. Her hands were shaking; indeed, her whole body trembled with an inner joy.

She stooped to the ground, unwrapped her bundle — and pulled out a live infant.

Behind her, the soldier yelled in outraged astonishment. The woman paid him no heed. With intense concentration, she bent over her baby. Nothing existed at that moment but the tiny boy, the sharp knife in her hand, and the covenant that she was about to sanctify between her son and her Maker, here in the valley of death in the shadow of the gas ovens.

She recited the blessing quietly, with devotion, her face alight. The Kapo approached from the side, watching incredulously. Saws stopped their motion. The Rebbe stood stock still, eyes closed in silent fervor.

"*Baruch attah … asher kidshanu b'mitzvosav v'tzivanu al hamilah.*"

Carefully wielding the knife, she cut the small piece of skin that had served as a barrier between her baby and his Father in Heaven.

Now that the deed was done, new life surged through the woman, even here, in the factory of death and despair. A new servant had been sworn in to the ranks of the King. Bowing as though in prayer, she said softly, "You gave me a kosher child, my Master, and I am returning to you a kosher child!"

Silently, she held out the knife, still dripping blood, to the Kapo. Then she placed her whimpering bundle into his arms.

The soldier stared into the baby's face, then at the knife. As though propelled by some unseen power, he placed the bundle gently on the ground, covered the baby with care, and wiped the knife on the hem of his coat. With his sleeve, he dashed a tear from his eye. Then he quickly left the scene.

One hour later, the woman was sent into the gas chamber holding her baby in her arms — two pure sacrifices.

Whenever the Bluzhever Rebbe would recount this, his entire body would tremble. Invariably, those listening to him recall this incident would dissolve in a sea of tears.

❧ The Scent of Freedom

In *Eretz Yisrael*, a gentle spring breeze carried the intoxicating fragrance of flowers — and fresh-baked matzah. Everything heralded the coming of the festival of freedom.

In Russia, the situation was very different. The atmosphere was icy and inhospitable, and the rivers ran crimson with blood. Mitzvah observance came along with a risk that was literally life threatening. Mrs. Gita Zilber had firsthand experience with this. She was one of those who sacrificed everything in order to keep the precious mitzvos and to educate her children in the Torah's ways.

The consequences of her choices soon became evident. Gita was fired from her job and subjected to K.G.B. interrogation. She was beaten and tortured, and she stood in imminent danger of death — but she was not afraid. She was living the way her G-d required her to live.

Gita's two young children were left alone for long hours, separated from their parents. Indeed, they had not seen their father for many days. He was in prison, paying his debt to society. His crime was labeled — in the words of the Communist regime — "dangerous incitement": In other words, he was an observant Jew. Gita was forced to be both mother and father to her children, and to worry about her husband at the same time. When not being persecuted by the K.G.B., she was working. She needed to earn a living for her family, while concealing the fact that her husband was behind bars. For who would wish to hire the wife of a criminal?

Pesach was approaching, but there was no scent of baking matzah in the air. Matzos were prepared secretly, in hidden rooms. The Communists recognized no Chosen People; indeed, they recognized no People at all, only a single nation of Soviet citizens. And yet, despite all the danger, it would never occur to these believing Jews to eat *chametz* on Pesach, or to neglect the mitzvah of eating matzah.

In a well-hidden room, the loyal Gita baked 50 pounds of matzah for her husband and all the Jewish prisoners incarcerated with him. Then she faced the real challenge: finding a way to transfer the matzos from her secret bakery to the lion's jaws — the Soviet prison.

She placed her treasury of well-wrapped matzos in a wheelbarrow, and proceeded to make her way along quiet side streets. Suddenly, a policeman accosted her.

"What do you have in that wheelbarrow?" he demanded.

"Why, they're cakes, in honor of my son's birthday," Gita answered serenely, praying inwardly that the officer remain deaf to the pounding of her heart.

The policeman looked skeptical. Gita hastened to explain.

"Sir, I am a schoolteacher. I have many students. I teach physics, but in the course of my studies I also learned how to be an electrical engineer. I work very hard, officer. Yesterday I spent hours cleaning the house. It's really sparkling today — "

This stream of talk was calculated to confuse the policeman — but the Soviet police do not confuse easily. The officer began beating Gita, and tried to drag her and her wheelbarrow away with him. She planted her feet in the frozen snow, trying not to think about what would happen if she, too, were thrown into prison. What would become of her children? And her husband — where would he get matzos for Pesach? As these fears whirled inside her head, Gita continued babbling in short, disjointed sentences.

The officer, losing patience with the stubborn woman, summoned another policeman to assist him. To his surprise, the second officer instructed him to let her go. Breathless at this unexpected reprieve, Gita hastened on her way. That day, with a great deal of Heavenly guidance, she succeeded in transferring the matzos to her husband and his fellow prisoners.

"Do you know who that second officer was?" Gita Zilber would end the story. "I'm positive that it was Eliyahu *HaNavi,* come to rescue me!"

❧ Two Documents, Two Signatures

Mrs. Recha Sternbuch's courage and character found expression as never before as the Nazi storm clouds were gathering over Europe. As Germany tightened its death grip on the Jews of that continent, Mrs. Sternbuch was indefatigable in her efforts to help save Jewish lives by smuggling them over the border into her own country, Switzerland. In the months before the outbreak of World War II she returned to Germany again and again, helping many Jews to make their escape. When refugees arrived in Switzerland without the necessary visas (which were virtually impossible to obtain), Mrs. Sternbuch hid them in her own home.

Inevitably, this information reached the ears of the police. Consequently, Mrs. Sternbuch was arrested.

Prison authorities exerted themselves to learn the names of Mrs. Sternbuch's colleagues in her work, especially the driver of the vehicle that transported the refugees across the border. She would languish in jail, the judge threatened, until she revealed the names they wanted. Mrs. Sternbuch replied staunchly: "You may keep me here forever, but you'll get no names from me."

When she was eventually released, the story spread throughout the country. A lawyer by the name of Dr. Imhof, leader of a political party, sent Mrs. Sternbuch a letter, along with a check for 100 Swiss francs. The letter said: "This is in appreciation of your courage in prison. Use the money to rescue more people."

When Reb Yitzchak and Recha Sternbuch learned that Torah scholars were living in Shanghai under difficult conditions, they founded a committee to lend assistance. The committee printed an appeal, which found its way to American shores as well: "Four hundred yeshivah *bachurim* and 26 families of rabbis from Mir, Telz and Lublin are living in Shanghai and learning Torah under conditions of extreme poverty." The American Jews heard the appeal and sent help. The *bnei Torah* in Shanghai were saved. The committee secretary was listed as Recha Sternbuch.

The Sternbuchs expanded their rescue efforts. The committee they had founded remained in operation throughout the war years, and succeeded in rescuing thousands of Jews. Mr. Musy, a prominent Swiss national and a personal friend of Himmler, was instrumental in inducing the Germans to release approximately 1200 Jews to Switzerland directly from the concentration camps at the height of the war. It was Reb

Yitzchak and Recha Sternbuch who sent Musy to Germany. There are still many people alive today who owe their lives to the efforts of the Sternbuchs' committee.

After the war, Recha Sternbuch turned her efforts in a different direction. Thousands of Jewish orphans remained scattered among the Gentiles. These were children whose parents had put them into their neighbors' hands in order to save their lives. Many were being brought up in Catholic monasteries. In France alone, several thousand Jews were held by "COSOR," a group headed by a priest. Was it possible to hope that Catholic priests would hand over these children to a Jewish organization?

Mrs. Sternbuch found a way. She negotiated an agreement whereby "COSOR" would transfer the Jewish children left in France to Mrs. Recha Sternbuch. The date of the contract was June 19, 1945. It was signed by the priest who headed "COSOR," and by Recha Sternbuch.

How did she do it? How did she get the Christian organization in France to agree to hand over thousands of Jewish children? The methods behind her achievement remain shrouded in mystery. What is clear is the indubitable fact that she did accomplish the impossible. There is the signed contract to prove it.

Not satisfied with this success, she traveled into Poland to rescue the thousands of children left there in monasteries and private homes. She sent them from Poland to Prague, where her husband was waiting to receive them. Another staggering victory for a truly extraordinary woman.

"Vatis'chak leyom acharon" — And she joyfully awaits the last day. If Recha Sternbuch presents those two documents to the Heavenly Court — the first appeal on behalf of the Shanghai yeshivah students, and the contract with the Christian "COSOR," both of which bear her signature — then joy will undoubtedly be her just reward.

A Jewish Kitchen

Mrs. Aliza Greenblatt was a familiar figure at the Jerusalem slaughterhouse on Thursdays. She would come bearing a chicken, newly purchased at the *shuk* in honor of the Shabbos.

Before permitting the *shochet* to slaughter the chicken, Mrs. Greenblatt would ask him to inspect his knife in front of her. Once he had done so and assured her that it was acceptable for *shechitah*, she would request a second opinion. Only after the second *shochet* agreed with the first that the knife bore not the slightest flaw would she agree to have her chicken slaughtered.

Leaving the slaughterhouse, she would direct her steps homeward. There she would pluck the chicken with her own hands, and split it open. At this point, her husband, Reb Avraham Baruch, would be called in to examine the innards and ascertain that there was no *kashrus* problem that might render the chicken unfit. Once he had done this, she would salt the chicken and rinse it. She would perform every step herself, not relying on others to be as punctilious as she was in this area. Her goal was that the food in her kitchen be exemplary in its standard of *kashrus*.

Mrs. Greenblatt ran her kitchen this way all her life. Even after her husband's passing, she continued to maintain the highest standards of *kashrus*. She was not prepared to take a single bite of a chicken that she herself had not *kashered;* even as a guest at her children's tables she would make sure to bring along a pot of her own chicken, *kashered* and prepared with her own hands.

Needless to say, this behavior had a profound impression on all who knew her. In this righteous Jewish housewife could be seen a sterling example of a truly loving meticulousness in the performance of the mitzvos.

Anticipation

The home of Rebbetzin Chaya Ruchama Kopshitz was characterized by a constant expectation of redemption. She kept a drum in her house, with which to greet *Mashiach*. The Rebbetzin took good care of the instrument, and was often heard saying that there would be a rejoicing with drums and dancing when the Final Redemption came, such as the rejoicing Miriam led after the splitting of the Red Sea.

Once, her son fell and cut his lip open. The Rebbetzin, having recently given birth, was unable to take the boy to the hospital to have his lip stitched, and a kind neighbor offered to take him. Before the two left for the hospital, the Rebbetzin abjured her neighbor: "Please make sure that they sew the lip neatly, so that it leaves no scar. My son is a *Kohen*, and we have to be careful that no blemish prevents him from performing the service in the *Beis HaMikdash*."

This was the way she lived all her days, with a complete faith that served as a glowing inspiration to everyone who knew her.

A Blast in the Wilderness

The Fasten family found themselves suddenly adrift in a strange sea. They were wandering through Uzbekistan, remembering all the adventures they had met with since deciding to pack their bags and flee.

They felt a pang at the thought of all they had left behind, and a great yearning for their friends who had remained in their native land. (This was before they knew about gas chambers and concentration camps.) But there was not much time for thinking, regrets, or vain longings. Chana Golda, the housewife, was concerned with a variety of urgent problems. It was necessary to find some food, quickly. The cupboard was bare. But even this was not as worrisome to her as the fact that it was just days until Rosh Hashanah. Where in this forsaken place would she be able to find a shofar?

Hope was dim, but not dead. Chana Golda trekked to the closest town. It was a long distance to walk. Fatigued, but still hopeful, she made her way to a rubbish heap on the outskirts of town. The stench was overpowering but she could not let that deter her. With fierce determination, she plowed in.

It felt as though the search took forever. Would she find what she was looking for, or had the journey been in vain?

Her heart pounded as she caught sight of something. Eagerly, she reached in — and pulled out a decaying ram's head from the heap. The animal it belonged to had been slaughtered days before. By Divine good fortune, the head was still there.

A strong wind sent the clouds scudding across the darkening sky above the barren valleys. Alone, intent on her work, a small, fragile-looking woman bent over a ram's head, scraping at the base of the horn with a piece of metal. As she worked she hummed a joyous melody of thanks to Hashem. She labored diligently at her task until it was crowned with success — and she held the ram's horn intact in her hand.

That year, the blasts of a shofar echoed through the streets of old Uzbekistan. That year, the small Jewish population did not have to forgo the cherished *mitzvah* that ushers in the New Year for Jews the world over.

Part Six:
Blessings

❧ A Different Slant

The city of P'shischa was noted for its great rebbe, R' Bunim, who enlightened the world with his wisdom and holiness. In that city lived Mirel, a righteous woman who was a good friend of R' Bunim's wife, Rivkaleh.

Mirel was the daughter of a well-known family, descending from R' Avraham *HaMaggid* of P'shischa, and she had also earned a reputation for wisdom in her own right. Her brother, the P'shischa *chassid,* R' Kalman Baum, had been nicknamed *Der Kluger Kalman* (Kalman the Clever). Likewise, her mother, Riva, had been famous for her shrewd mind. People would bring her their problems and questions, certain to receive a sensible solution in return.

Apart from her sharp mind and illustrious family, Mirel was also possessed of considerable amounts of property in the city. She herself ran the family business, while her husband busied himself with Torah and *Chassidus*. He was a disciple of the *rebbeim* of Vorka. The blessing she once received from the old Rebbe, R' Yitzchak of Vorka, was Mirel's most cherished treasure. This is how it came about.

When she heard that the *Tzaddik* of Vorka was about to arrive in P'shischa, Mirel immediately walked toward the city limits to wait for him. Spotting his entourage approaching, she planted herself in the middle of the road so that the horses were forced to halt.

The Rebbe asked, "What does this woman want?"

They told him that she requested his blessing for a good livelihood.

The Rebbe turned to the woman and said, "Conduct your business honestly, and you will have a livelihood." And, indeed, from that moment Mirel's business flourished.

But there was still one thing that distressed her deeply. Many years passed, and the holy Reb Bunim had returned his soul to his Maker, but Mirel had not yet given birth to a child. One day, she shared her bitter disappointment with her friend, Rebbetzin Rivkaleh. The Rebbetzin shared fully in her pain, and promised to travel with her to see a disciple of her husband, the Kotzker Rebbe, to ask for his help.

Presently, the Kotzker Rebbe's door was closed to the public. For weeks, no *chassid* had entered the Rebbe's room. The *beis midrash* was filled with *chassidim*, devoting themselves to Hashem's work while awaiting word from their Rebbe. But all doors were open to the Rebbetzin from P'shischa. Immediately upon her arrival, she was ushered into the great Rebbe's room.

The Rebbetzin stood on one side of the room while outside, on the other side of the open door, stood Mirel, trembling with fear and hope. The Rebbe tilted his head, looked down at the floor, and asked the Rebbetzin the reason for her visit.

"I have brought a friend with me — a friend who needs help."

"And what does she want?"

"She wants to merit having children."

The Rebbe lifted a hand and said, "She will have countless children."

Mirel left the Rebbe's home in a state of euphoria still tinged with fear. She had heard the Rebbe's promise with her own ears. There was no doubt in her mind that her salvation was near.

Years passed, with no sign of a child. Still, Mirel clung to her belief in the *tzaddik's* words. Her salvation would come in its proper time.

Upon the passing of his rebbe, R' Menachem Mendel of Vorka, Mirel's husband, R' Chaim Hirsch Mendel, traveled to see R' Berish, the Rebbe of Biala, to plead for a son. The Rebbe reminded him of a famous *segulah*: writing a conditional divorce. The document would state that he would divorce his wife if she did not bear children during the coming year. R' Chaim Hirsch went home and told his wife what the Rebbe had advised.

Mirel refused to consider it. She was still certain that the Kotzker Rebbe's blessing would bear fruit. Upon hearing of her refusal, the Biala Rebbe asked her to come see him.

"Why won't you agree to try this *segulah*, which may help you bear children?"

Mirel replied, "I already have the Kotzker Rebbe's promise."

The Biala Rebbe was surprised. "If that's the case, you will certainly have the salvation you wish for. Tell me, what were his words?"

When he heard the wording of the Kotzker Rebbe's blessing, the Biala Rebbe sighed. "You will not have children. It is impossible to merit 'countless' children. The Rebbe was referring to what *Chazal* say about teaching Torah to other people's offspring, or raising orphans in your home: These children are considered as being born to you. In this way, it is possible to have 'countless' children. This is what you should begin doing."

Mirel listened, nodded her head and began to make her peace with this possibility.

From that day on, Mirel paid tutition fees for poor children. She also kept a special room in her house for storing clothes and other wedding necessities for poor brides and grooms who could not afford their own. She would supply everything they needed to marry and start life together.

It was the custom of R' Simcha Bunim, the Otovosk Rebbe, to stay with R' Chaim Hirsch and Mirel whenever he was in P'shischa. On one such visit, he inadvertently went into the room Mirel kept for the orphans. The room was filled with pillows and blankets, in preparation for a poor bride's wedding.

Surprised, R' Simcha Bunim asked for an explanation. When told of the room's purpose, he said, "In that case, they will have a warm spot in the Higher World."

Mirel's *chesed* was recorded on her tombstone. The chiseled words read: "With her own hands, she married off 36 poor orphans."

❧ The Orphan

Chaya Ruchama Shenker lost her mother at the age of 9. As the oldest girl in the family, the burden of running the house fell squarely on her young shoulders. It was no easy feat to relinquish, in a single day, the carefree joys of childhood, and to take up the cares of housewifery. But reality imposes things upon us, whether we choose them or not. This was Chaya Ruchama's fate.

As the girl grew, so did her aspirations. Her father was the *tzaddik*, R' Shmuel Shenker, son-in-law of R' Yosef Chaim Sonnenfeld. Chaya Ruchama's heart burned with ambition to lead a Torah life, and when the time came for her to marry, she asked that she be wed to a great man, a man who would devote all of his time to Torah. This would comfort her for the childhood she had lost.

When an outstanding young man, R' Tzvi Kopshitz, was suggested for her, she quickly saw that this was a man with whom she could build the kind of home of which she dreamed. They became engaged. But, as the wedding date grew near, it became apparent that there was not enough money for her dowry — not even the requisite minimum. Conditions were very difficult in Jerusalem at that time.

In desperation, Chaya Ruchama turned to her grandfather, the great R' Yosef Chaim Sonnenfeld, Jerusalem's rabbi. He maintained a fund for needy families, brides and grooms. Out of this fund he would provide pillows and blankets. Confident that she would be able to receive at least what any other indigent bride was offered, Chaya Ruchama asked her grandfather for what she needed.

R' Yosef Chaim answered, "My daughter, since I started this fund it has been my policy never to give money from it to my family and relatives. I cannot give you what I am able to give others."

The girl was astonished and crestfallen. Speechless, she gazed at the man upon whom she had pinned all her hopes. R' Yosef Chaim looked at her and said, "In order not to deprive you of the accepted dowry, I will give you my own pillow and blanket."

Chaya Ruchama refused to countenance this. "I cannot agree, under any circumstances. I will remain dowryless, but I won't take your pillow and blanket from you, Zeide."

R' Yosef Chaim's eyes lit up. He gazed at his granddaughter with a mixture of pity and joy. "You should know that *Adam HaRishon* had no bedding, either."

Swiftly she answered, "That is true, Grandfather. Adam had no bedding — but his sons did."

R' Yosef Chaim smiled at the clever girl and blessed her, "In the merit of your declining my offer, your sons will all be *talmidei chachamim*."

Chaya Ruchama left his home feeling that she had received far more than a simple dowry. She had received a blessing that her offspring would be Torah scholars. Could there be anything more important than that?

The blessing came true. She had 11 sons and sons-in-law, every one of them an outstanding Torah scholar — all the fruits of this wonderful woman's labor to instill in her offspring her own love of Torah and her desire to grow in its ways.

✌ Changing Fortunes

R' Aryeh Leib, author of the *Sha'agas Aryeh*, founded a yeshivah in Minsk. Over time, the yeshivah became a magnet that drew great numbers of aspiring students, eager to learn at the great Rabbi's feet.

There were, however, those who disagreed so vehemently with the opinions of the Sha'agas Aryeh that he was forced to leave Minsk.

The locals rented a simple horse and wagon for R' Aryeh Leib and his wife. In scorn and ridicule they saw the wagon past the town limits, with no thought for the fact that it was Friday afternoon. Because of their precipitate departure, the Rabbi and Rebbetzin would have to spend Shabbos in a field or a forest.

Among the crowd seeing them off was a woman who sold bread and Shabbos candles for a living. She was filled with pity for the Rabbi and his wife. Pushing her way through the throng, her heavy baskets on her arm, she gave R' Aryeh Leib candles and three challos for Shabbos.

R' Aryeh Leib was deeply moved by this act of simple kindness. From the depths of his heart he blessed the woman: "Hashem will repay you, my daughter, as you deserve, with riches and honor."

Before long, the woman had indeed grown prosperous, and her every effort was crowned with success. R' Aryeh Leib had bestowed the same "blessing" on the city of Minsk: "Hashem will repay you as you deserve." From time to time, conflagrations would erupt in the city, punishing those who had sinned against the great man.

When the couple arrived in a neighboring town, a villager had pity on them and invited them into his home. He cleared a room for them in the attic, where they slept on straw on the floor.

Gradually, R' Aryeh Leib recovered from his ordeal. With his usual fervor, he returned to his learning. One night, after their simple meal, he sat with his Gemara by the feeble light of a kerosene lamp. For some time the tiny attic room was quiet as he pored over a *sugyah* with total concentration. Suddenly, he was struck by a wonderful idea. He had thought of a whole new approach to the *sugyah*, one which would resolve all his questions and doubts. His face glowed with joy, and his eyes beamed with pleasure and thanksgiving to Hashem for this gift.

The Rebbetzin was seated opposite him, busy with her own work. Witnessing her husband's happiness, she felt a joyous sense of satisfaction of her own. But when she met his eyes, she was shocked to see that her husband's eyes were damp with tears!

Anxiously, she asked, "Leib, why are you crying?"

In a sad voice, R' Aryeh Leib answered, "Look how good we have it today. We ate, we drank, we're sitting in a lighted room and have a place to sleep. We are enjoying the peace and quiet and taking pleasure in the Torah. How it worries me! Are we receiving our reward now instead of in the next world?"

✄ Blumka

During the days when the Sha'agas Aryeh was *Rosh Yeshivah* in Minsk, there was a righteous woman living there whose name was Blumka Willenkin. She helped support the *tzaddik* with money and food. She built him a special study hall, which was known until World War II as *"Blumka's Kloiz"* (Blumka's *beis midrash*). It was there that R' Chaim Volozhiner later opened his yeshivah, where many of the world's most noted scholars served as *Roshei Yeshivah*. Throughout, the supporting hand was always Blumka's.

It is said that the Sha'agas Aryeh bestowed a blessing on the woman, saying that she would merit building one shul in Minsk and another in *Eretz Yisrael*. Many years later, as she was approaching old age, Blumka was seized with the desire to fulfill the *tzaddik's* prediction and move to *Eretz Yisrael*. Before she made her decision, however, she consulted with R' Chaim Volozhiner. To move, or not?

R' Chaim's answer was eminently logical. "Since you already have the Sha'agas Aryeh's blessing in your bag, why hurry to leave now? Who knows how long you will live afterwards? He promised that you will build a shul in Eretz Yisrael. It is better, then, to wait and see how things work out."

Blumka took the Rabbi's advice and remained in Minsk. Only years later, when she had achieved a remarkably advanced age, did she finally make the trip to *Eretz Yisrael*, where she built a shul, just as the Sha'agas Aryeh had foretold.

Immediately after the completion of the building, Blumka joined her ancestors.

✎ A Mixed Blessing

Seventeen years had passed since Toba Wishniak's wedding day — 17 years without offspring. The righteous woman redoubled her prayers and visited all the Torah greats of Poland with a single request: to be blessed with children. She was prepared to give anything to achieve her heart's desire.

Her travels took her to Poland where a *tzaddik* listened to her plea in silence. Finally, he responded, "But you won't raise him."

Bravely, Toba said, "Even so." He blessed her, and within the year she gave birth to a son.

In great joy and gratitude, the radiant mother began preparing for the *bris*. With her own hands she made certain it would be a true celebration. The occasion would be both a *seudas mitzvah* and a feast of thanksgiving for having glimpsed her reward in her lifetime.

Guests attended the *bris* from all parts of the city. There was an atmosphere of genuine rejoicing among the many who thronged to participate. Toba herself had glowed with a special feeling: She had merited adding a new link in the chain of her illustrious family.

Just three days later, the new mother returned her soul to her Maker, leaving her infant behind. She had not merited to be the one to have the privilege of raising him. But she *had* succeeded in contributing her share to the continuation of the Jewish people through the ages.

❧ The Washerwoman

A modest woman would visit the home of R' Shloimele of Zevhil each week. It was Miriam's job to wash the household laundry. Diligently and faithfully she scrubbed one article of clothing after another. She washed and bleached and rinsed, deeming it an honor to serve the Rebbe and his family in this way.

Miriam was a pious woman, filled with a burning desire to fulfill Hashem's will. Every Monday and Thursday she fasted, and in the month of Elul she fasted every day. She labored over the laundry as though it were a great privilege, as indeed she considered it to be.

But even in moments of happiness, there was always a touch of sadness lurking in Miriam's eyes. She had no children. She had never complained about this source of pain, and refrained even from referring to her bitter lot. After a number of years of working in the Rebbe's house, however, she finally decided to ask him to intercede on her behalf with his prayers.

Accordingly, one day when she had completed her work, Miriam came to stand in the Rebbe's doorway. "Please, Rebbe, bless me with children!"

The Rebbe remained lost in his thoughts for several minutes. Finally he told her, "I cannot help you."

The answer froze Miriam's tired body. After a brief pause, the rebbe continued, "I bless you in this: that your merit shall bring salvation to others."

Miriam carried the Rebbe's words in her heart for years, until her death in 5724 (1964). Her passing left no impression on the Jerusalem community in which she had lived. She did not even have a son to recite *Kaddish* for her. She died alone, a widow, and was buried quietly on Har HaMenuchos. The washerwoman's simple tombstone merely gave her name and the date of her death.

Twenty-nine years later, in 5753 (1993), a former neighbor of hers told an intriguing tale. Miriam had appeared to her in a dream and said, "I used to wash the clothes at the home of Reb Shloimele of Zevhil. I had no children, and asked the Rebbe for his blessing. He could not help me, he said, but his blessing was for others to be through me.

"It is time for holy souls to descend to this world, and I ask that prayers be said at my grave for the benefit of my soul. I promise that barren women who do this will be cured. Here are instructions for finding my grave ..."

The woman related the dream to a friend of hers, who spread it further. It eventually reached a women's group in Jerusalem, who decided to try to find the grave of Miriam the washerwoman. They went to the cemetery at Har HaMenuchos, where — with the help of the explicit directions given in the dream — they found Miriam's grave among the tens of thousands scattered over the mountain.

On Sunday, the 24th day of Teves 5753 (1993), the paths of Har HaMenuchos were clogged with a vast crowd. One after another, buses rolled up to deposit more and more visitors. They had all come to the grave of the widow Miriam.

A young yeshivah man stood by the grave, emotionally reciting *Kaddish* for the washerwoman's soul. The crowd responded in a roar. Tears stole down many cheeks, and many sad tales were spilled over the grave that had become, overnight, a symbol of hope for barren women.

The beseeching prayers to Hashem on behalf of the deceased woman were rewarded. That same year, in Jerusalem, 32 previously barren woman gave birth! As clear and bright as the candles that line the expanded and renovated gravesite is this testimony to a righteous woman, who served Hashem with devotion all her life, and who ended by becoming a spokesperson for the suffering before the very Throne of Glory.

Part Seven:
Women in Education

📌 The Birth of Bais Yaakov

FAMILY PRESSURES FORCED SARAH SCHENIERER TO earn her living as a seamstress. Carefully and patiently, she sewed fashionable dresses for women and girls. As her machine whirred, so did her thoughts.

She would remember the words of R' Hirsch of Riminov: "I was a tailor's apprentice. I always tried to mend the old clothes and not to ruin the new." But here, in Sarah Schenierer's opinion, the new were already being ruined. How assiduously the women toiled over their patterns, colors and styles. Heaven forbid that a seam should emerge crooked! But were they equally concerned, the seamstress wondered, with their spiritual garb? Were they as anxious to find favor in Heaven's eyes as they were to appear to advantage in human ones?

The situation, she decided, was not good. A new pattern must be cut — from our own holy tradition.

World War One broke out. Sarah Schenierer and her family fled to Vienna, Austria, where they found the Jewish ghetto too crowded to accommodate yet another family of refugees. They were forced to live in the Gentile quarter of the city.

It was here, unexpectedly, that salvation arrived. Searching for a shul in which to *daven* on Shabbos, she came upon an interesting lecturer. Rabbi Moshe David Flesch, a student of Rabbi Saloman Breuer, the son-in-law and successor of the late Rabbi Samson Raphael Hirsch, sprinkled his talk with pearls of Rabbi Hirsch's wisdom.

Sarah Schenierer sat spellbound through his lectures. The speaker's words seemed to reflect the very thoughts churning inside her own heart. Her private musings were presented with marvelous new clarity. She began an extensive course of readings in the works of Rabbi Hirsch, Rabbi Lehman and others who had defined the nature of Judaism and instilled a genuine Jewish pride in their readers. *"Koh somar l'bais Yaakov"* — "Thus shall you say to the House of Jacob." The words reverberated in her mind.

Another verse echoed there, too: *"Bais Yaakov lechu v'neilchah be'or Hashem"* — "House of Jacob, go forward in Hashem's light." In Hashem's light — that was the way. Just 30 years earlier a movement had arisen, calling itself "BILU," an acronym for *"Bais Yaakov Lechu V'neilchah."* That movement did not go forward in Hashem's light, however. Instead it led its members to secular Zionism, to life without the yoke of Torah. There was now a need to establish a truly Jewish movement — in Hashem's light. A movement of girls, proud of their Jewish heritage. And what was a more fitting name for this movement than "Bais Yaakov"? In the verse, "Thus shall you say to the House of Jacob *(Bais Yaakov)* and relate to the Children of Israel," "Bais Yaakov" refers to the women. It was necessary to find new ways to instruct Jewish girls in Torah and Judaism, and to weave the eternal truths into their everyday lives.

The notion was born. The name was found. But implementing it was still only a dream. Sarah Schenierer plied her scissors on old articles of clothing, and the wheels of her sewing machine still spun busily as she refashioned them into pretty new dresses for poor girls.

Things continued in this way until the right hour struck. When Sarah Schenierer returned to Cracow after the war, she delivered a series of lectures to girls, in Yiddish. At first, the sight of the modestly dressed woman, speaking not Polish or German but the Yiddish vernacular, gave rise to more than one raised eyebrow among those listening. But Sarah Schenierer never despaired of success. Her goal was crystal-clear: "We must establish a school for young girls, for these tender flowers. Then strong trees will grow — trees that no wind will succeed in uprooting."

With this thought in mind, she set to work. She hung a sign on her door: "Here we educate girls in *limudei kodesh*." It did not take long for her to gather 25 young students. Twenty-five is equivalent to the numerical value of *"koh"* ("Thus") in *"Koh somar l'bais Yaakov."* Within the four walls of her own home, she began to teach the children Torah.

Sometimes, the loftiest ideas can be the simplest ones. When Sarah Schenierer put her brilliant plan into practice, people began to say, "Of course — it's so elementary. Why didn't we think of this before?" Sarah Schenierer's school was based on a fundamental concept, a natural notion, a revolutionary idea. Apart from the mockers and the skeptics, there rose a strong body of genuinely zealous Jews who were afraid of overturning a longstanding tradition. They feared the introduction of change. But Sarah Schenierer, staunch in her faith, declared: "Whatever the Torah leaders tell me, that is what I'll do."

Together with her esteemed brother, who was both a rabbi and a *dayan*, she traveled to the Belzer Rebbe, then vacationing in the health spa at Marienbad. Her brother entered the Rebbe's room and wrote: "She wants to guide and instruct Jewish girls in Torah and *Yiddishkeit* ..." The holy Rebbe read the note, and responded with great warmth, *"Berachah v'hatzlachah"* ("Blessings and success").

These words had an electrifying effect on Sarah. In her journal, she wrote, "They influenced me like a wonderful elixir of life, infusing me with an invigorating energy. The great *tzaddik's* blessing has given me full confidence in the fulfillment of my dream."

But there was still opposition to contend with. A group of people went to the Chofetz Chaim, who was well advanced in years by that time, with an outcry: "Has such a thing ever been heard of — a school for Jewish girls?" The Chofetz Chaim lit up as though he had uncovered a vast treasure, and exclaimed, "Praiseworthy is the one who thought up such a good idea! It is a pity I was not a part of it."

R' Meir Shapiro of Lublin extended the idea even further, encouraging the establishment of a teachers' seminary. He wanted Bais Yaakov graduates to study educational methodology, to enable them to spread the Bais Yaakov movement to all parts of Europe.

Sarah Schenierer and her fledgling school were blessed with Heavenly assistance. Her novel idea was quickly accepted by the majority of the populace. The Agudath Israel movement undertook to support first the schools and then the seminary. What began in a small, dim room, where the girls took notes on their laps for lack of desks, soon snowballed into something stupendous. From every small town — places where organized Torah education for girls had been undreamed of — came pious fathers with a plea for Sarah Schenierer: "Send us teachers!" At their own expense they rented meager apartments and supported the sole teacher, who was also the school's acting principal and janitor. Sarah Schenierer herself devised the teaching curriculum.

In those places where the town fathers did not take the initiative to start a school, Sarah Schenierer came to them, to coax and plead and persuade. Her first step in any new town was always to address the women and girls. In simple, clear language that came straight from the heart, she would ask, "Will you not invest in your precious flowers? What will you do when a fine yeshivah *bachur* is suggested as a husband for your daughter, and she turns up her fine, Polish-educated nose and says she'd rather have a 'cultured' young man?"

The dedicated educator traveled from city to city, from community to community, spreading her influence wherever she went. It is impossible to state categorically what her magic was. It was not her external appearance, nor was it an especially gifted tongue. But people listened to her as though mesmerized. Every word pierced their hearts until they were determined to do as she asked.

Each time a fledgling teacher came to start a school in a new town, Sarah Schenierer accompanied her. She would inspect the premises and the surroundings, pouring some of her own confidence into the young woman and injecting her own special brand of goodness into the atmosphere.

Bais Yaakov came a long way in a short time. In the year 5677 (1917), Sarah Schenierer had founded the first school with 25 students; seven years later, there were 54 schools in Poland, catering to thousands of students. The time had come to erect a permanent building.

"This silver coin is the first donation for the seminary building to be built for Bais Yaakov teachers." With these words, a Cracow Jew, enthusiastic about Sarah Schenierer and her accomplishments, started the fund. Sarah Schenierer kept that coin as a symbol of trust and hope. And that trust was borne out. In the year 5693 (1933), she witnessed the completion of a seminary building for older girls — a beautiful, five-story structure capable of holding 120 students.

When the cornerstone was laid, Sarah Schenierer buried the coin with it. Her dream had come true.

❧ Who Was Batya?

She was always known as Sarah Schenierer's right hand. When the first seminary was opened, she was the *limudei kodesh* teacher. She was present at meetings with the Torah giants of the time, including R' Chaim Ozer Grodzinski, and the Gerrer Rebbe, and was involved in devising curricula and methodologies for drawing Jewish girls toward a traditional Jewish education. The young woman was Batya Rothschild, the spirit that breathed life into the Cracow seminary. She had been recruited from Switzerland — already a successful teacher — to help establish the mighty edifice that Bais Yaakov promised to become.

The two met through the good offices of Dr. Leo Deutschlander, one of the leaders of Germany's Jewish community. In the year 5675 (1915) he visited Cracow, in Poland, and witnessed Sarah Schenierer's efforts at founding Bais Yaakov in that city. Quickly seeing that she needed an assistant, he sent to Switzerland for Batya Rothschild. From the moment she stepped over the school's threshold, Batya devoted all her abilities to the furtherance of Bais Yaakov.

Among her activities were gatherings on Friday nights and Shabbos afternoons. These get-togethers helped strengthen the girls to withstand the foreign winds that were blowing through Europe at that time, giving them a solid Torah perspective on life. It is interesting that it was these meetings, outside of the school curriculum, which drew many girls closer to Batya in admiration and deep affection.

At the founding meeting, over 300 girls signed on as members of the Shabbos activity group. These hundreds appeared regularly, week after week, absorbing the very roots of *Yiddishkeit* with each meeting.

Marriage forced Batya to leave Poland and settle in Germany. As a mark of their respect and esteem, the hundreds of girls who had organized to meet every Shabbos decided to name their group after her. From then on, it was called "Batya."

The years passed. Batya used them well, weaving a wonderful tapestry of life through her personality and many activities. She passed away in the year 5750 (1990), at the age of 90.

At every stage of her life, she maintained a close bond with Sarah Schenierer, and until her dying day Batya kept the *Mishlo'ach Manos* that Sarah Schenierer had sent her, along with her picture.

The most extraordinary thing is that Mrs. Batya Rothschild Baumgarten left this world on *Erev Shabbos*, the 26th day of Adar: exactly the same date, day of the week, and hour as Sarah Schenierer.

❧ Like the Waves

"Life is like the waves of the sea. Duck your head to let each passing wave wash over you, and then stand upright again ... Yes, I have ducked my head many times in my life, and Hashem has saved me from all of it ..."

Thus wrote Massouda Cohen in her diary on the 19th day of Kislev 5737 (1977).

For 49 years Massouda Cohen climbed a continuously upward path, battling many obstacles — both spiritual and physical — on her way until her soul returned to its Maker on the fifth day of Adar I 5749 (1989).

Who was this remarkable woman?

Tiberias, 5700 (1940). It was a stormy time, a time of Jewish persecution by the Arabs. Violence and murder in *Eretz Yisrael* had become routine. It was summer, and the sun scorched unrelentingly. Because of the heat and the fear, many people slept on their rooftops. On one such night, Mrs. Maatuka Cohen, a wise and good woman, returned from the hospital with her newborn baby, Massouda. The baby cried incessantly. Neighbors, hearing the infant's wails, climbed up to the Cohens' roof to see if they could help calm her.

Suddenly, there was a mighty blast. The house next door — the house that the neighbors had just left — exploded. The lives of these neighbors had been saved because of that baby. It was the first *chesed* on record that Massouda performed for her fellow man.

Tiberias was fighting for its spiritual identity. Those of the old school, living in the shadow of R' Akiva, R' Meir Ba'al HaNess, the Rambam and all the other luminaries buried in its soil, were engaged in a bitter battle with proponents of the more modern winds blowing through Israel at the time, brought there by the new settlers. These newcomers wanted to eradicate the old Tiberias and place the stamp of youth on the city.

Despite the final hardship, Massouda's parents sent her to the local Bais Yaakov, where the girl graduated with honors. While her friends went on to continue their studies in faraway Bnei Brak, the Cohens were too poor to provide this opportunity for their daughter. Against her will, the realities of life forced Massouda to take up vocational training in secretarial skills. This was to be her first test.

There was much to contend with: on the one hand prejudice and mockery, and on the other, forces aimed at conquering the spirit of Sephardic Jews like Massouda. The 14-year-old faced her challenges with courage, insistent on maintaining her modest dress and innocent ways. As she wrote in her diary:

> *"In the shul near our house I cried many tears ... Ribono Shel Olam! Help me walk in Your ways, help me to not become ruined. Please — help me be strong!"*

Once, while working in a secular office, Massouda recorded the following plea in her diary:

> Forgive me, my Father and King. I am working in a place that is so secular, so far from knowing You, that they keep fighting me about my long sleeves, my stockings, the length of my skirt. I can't take it anymore!

With steely determination, Massouda left her job and traveled away from her birthplace, heading for the Bais Yaakov high school in Bnei Brak.

She completed her studies there, too with honors. During those years, her goal became clear: to teach! She sensed that her life's work was to influence Jewish girls with a message that came from the depths and purity of her own heart.

Rabbi Wolf's high school offered her a job, but she knew where her true mission lay. It was the girls of Sephardic extraction that needed her most. She turned, therefore, to a different girls' school, the "Ohr HaChaim." It was more than just a job, more than merely a means to earn her living. For Massouda, it was the essence of her life.

With her dedication and single-mindedness, is it any wonder that she rose to the position of school principal? A glance into her diary speaks volumes about the energy and enthusiasm she brought to her sacred work, as well as her extraordinary modesty. On the day she was appointed principal, she wrote:

> 13 Elul 5731 (1971). Today they cleared out the office assigned to me. They're calling me 'principal,' a title that fills me with sadness and shame. I don't know if I deserve that title … It carries with it an obligation. Unfortunately, the world is concerned only with impressions and external titles. Still, in this way it will be easier to achieve the goals set forth by our fathers! May it be Your Will, my L-rd, that I succeed in my work, for the sake of Your service and Your glory.

Despite her tender heart and her love for her students, Massouda knew how to stand firm. With the Torah greats of the generation guiding her, she fixed her course and clung to it. Once, with the rabbis' approval, she established a uniform for her girls. This generated a great deal of discontent among the students, who did not like the idea at all. The principal sympathized, but would not be swayed from her position. Beautiful clothes are not a Jewish girl's true adornment, she would say; *tznius* is what lends her a genuine charm. And so, although the school taught sewing, she insisted that its corridors were not the proper showcase for the results. Modest, clean clothing was good enough.

Further excerpts from her diary:

> *I am now fully engaged in my responsible work. I must make decisions about when to discipline and when to grant pardon to the girls, conduct discussions with the teachers, etc. I am filled with a single prayer: 'May it be Your Will that I speak and act intelligently ... and may the merit of the many stand in my behalf, as I have neither the physical strength nor the financial reserves for the burdens laid upon me ...'*
> *... Today was a very hard and busy day. It seemed to me that a number of teachers were insulted by my demands — but You, Master of the Universe, know that I did nothing, and do nothing, except for the salvation of the precious Jewish girls knocking on Ohr HaChaim's door, so that they may be illuminated with the light of true life!*

In 5739 (1979), Massouda Cohen became ill with a heart disease and had to travel abroad for an operation. Her diary attests to her suffering, and also to the spiritual elevation that her suffering brought about. Massouda accepted the ordeal with love and faith, never abandoning her deepest hope, "to return to my country, to my family and to my dear girls at Ohr HaChaim ..."

Friday, the 10th of Adar, was the day scheduled for her surgery. From her sickbed, she wrote:

> *It is nearly Purim today in our holy land. I feel an intense longing for the sweet children in their costumes. The joy of Purim! Where was I yesterday — and where today? Then, the joy of Purim filled the entire house. Who will give money to the poor today, and who will send the Mishlo'ach Manos? But everything is for the best! How to put it? The sufferings I've undergone are not something I would exchange, because they will serve as atonement for my sins, and in the future. I want nothing more. Master of the Universe, give me health, and renew my strength so that I may serve You in awe, in the name of Heaven …*

Just before the operation, she penned the following words:

> *May it be Your Will, Master of the Universe, that anyone who thinks I've wronged them will forgive me … because I had no intention of hurting any person … but I know that there are those who were hurt because of my educational aims and because of my desire for truth.*
> *I did it not for my own honor nor for the honor of my family. The truth guided me. There may have been gaps in my understanding, but my intentions were always l'shem Shamayim. I have forgiven them all long ago. May Hashem forgive all my sins …*

For three weeks, Massouda struggled with the Angel of Death, until Hashem granted her renewed life. Her diary is filled with the experience, radiant with gratitude despite all her suffering. During that period, the 19th of Adar, she wrote:

> *How manifold are Your kindnesses, Hashem, Who has not abandoned us and will not abandon us! There are angels from on high to greet us everywhere. Always there is some-*

one ready to explain, to advise, to help, to smooth our way, and everything is waiting for us as though we were beloved only sons. Praise Hashem, for He is good, for His lovingkindness is eternal! "For You were a stronghold for the meek, a stronghold for the destitute when he was in distress ..." (Yeshayahu 25:4).

And, just before leaving the hospital to return home in Iyar of that same year:

My country, my beautiful country, wonderful Eretz Yisrael, I'm on my way to you, to my family, to my friends. Is the day really so close? An end to my wanderings, to my anguish, to my pain! I feel like singing! Celebrating! I am all happiness — but as for strength, I have none. Praise Hashem, for He is good!

Upon recovering from the surgery, she returned to work, where she was eventually rewarded with the crowning fulfillment of all her efforts: an expansion of Ohr HaChaim to include a seminary of studies for girls of Sephardic extraction. She paid loving attention to the smallest of details: to the pictures on the walls, to flowers, to everything and anything that might help make the place a true educational home for her girls. This was her *nachas*!

Did Massouda sense that her days were numbered? What was it that drove her all the time, to organize, to act, to help, to build an edifice to eternity?

On the other side of the coin of her marvelous educational work was the caring that was ever in the forefront of her consciousness. Any pained or bitter heart received a hearing; any needy sufferer found an open door. Discovering, to her sorrow, that the ranks of the needy were numerous, she founded an organization which she named "*Eishes Chayil.*" The organization provided meals for needy families, help to new mothers, money for the destitute and clothing for brides.

Through diligent effort, she reached poor and suffering people whose existence was unknown to any but herself. She conducted all the organization's affairs with remarkable efficiency, so that when government accountants came to audit its books, they marveled at the exactitude and order with which she had handled the accounts.

At her funeral and afterwards, many tales of kindness came to light — wonderful acts of *chesed* such as restoring harmony to the home and bringing succor to the brokenhearted — so that everyone who had thought they knew Massouda Cohen discovered that they knew only a fraction of her many facets. How had she managed it all herself, and with her dwindling strength?

He who accepts suffering with love will be rewarded greatly. During the years of her pain, Massouda rose to great heights. She suffered, but she did not succumb to suffering: She fought it with active heroism. Each small triumph nurtured her with new hope and raised her spiritual level yet a notch higher.

In the final weeks of her life, when members of her household wished to put a sign on the door asking visitors to refrain from coming to see her because of her weakened state, Massouda objected strenuously. Perhaps there was someone out there who needed her? Someone who might benefit from a bit of advice, a good word, a smile?

> *… So often, you will hear: 'I don't want to listen to other people's troubles; my own are enough for me.' I've heard this more than once, and how it has pained my heart … Shall I be unwilling to listen to others, too? Heaven forbid! Master of the Universe, give me the strength to listen and to help my fellow man — because it was for this that we were created …*

Indeed, this was what Massouda had been created for. In her last days, she told her family: "I am calm. I have prepared a dowry for that orphaned bride."

Doubled over with agonizing pain, readying herself for her

final journey to the hospital — the journey from which she would not return — she asked her husband to hurry and provide financial support for two poor families before Shabbos.

After weeks of suffering, when at last her strength failed her and she was no longer able to extend a hand, Massouda returned her soul to its Maker. She stands as an example for anyone who has ever suffered — an example of triumph over adversity at any cost.

Part Eight:
Lovingkindness

❦ Small Deeds, Great Rewards

It was dusk, and another day in Vilna was winding down. Laborers and shopkeepers were making their way to the *beis midrash*, to spend a sweet hour side by side with *bnei Torah*.

Two women were going on their way through the streets of Vilna. They were the Vilna Gaon's wife and her friend. Throughout the day they had been knocking on doors, raising money for an indigent bride so that she might be wed in a respectable fashion. This charitable quest was urgent, as the match itself depended on it. Whenever the women's energy began to flag, they would remind themselves of the important mitzvah in which they were engaged and doggedly continue on.

As dusk fell, they caught sight of one of the town's wealthy woman. Eagerly, they waved at her to wait. Rushing up to where she was standing, they poured out the tale of the poor, orphaned bride. The rich woman pledged a generous donation.

Reaching the end of their day's work at last, the two friends prepared to separate. As they stood together for a last few minutes, their conversation turned to spiritual matters. One of the things they discussed was the World to Come. Out of this came a mutual pledge: The first of them to depart this world would visit the other within 30 days of her passing, to describe Heaven's doings to the friend left behind.

And so it came to pass. When one of them died, she kept her promise and came back to her friend three days later. It was forbidden, she explained, to describe the World to Come. But there was one thing she was permitted to tell. The wave of their hands, as they had signaled the rich woman to wait so that they could solicit charity from her, had been duly recorded in Heaven — and its reward was very great indeed.

🍂 Looking Out for Number Two

When Rabbi Yechiel Mordechai Gordon's daughter became engaged, the bride's family promised to provide the sum of $500 toward the wedding expenses. Rabbi Gordon, in London at the time, sent his daughter a letter saying that upon his arrival in the United States he would do his best to borrow the money so that the wedding need not be postponed.

His daughter immediately sent her reply. Reading it, Rabbi Gordon was deeply moved. In the letter, his daughter described a friend of hers who was in dire straits. This friend, too, had recently become engaged, but it looked like the match would be broken off. The $500 that the girl's father had promised as her dowry had been lent to a yeshivah, and the yeshivah, in difficult financial circumstances, found itself unable to pay back its debt.

"Therefore," Rabbi Gordon's daughter concluded, "both my *chasan* and I wish to ask you, dear father, to take the money you were planning to raise for us, and to send it to my friend. The two of us will make do with what we have."

The letter touched the hearts of everyone who read it. Word of its contents reached his friend, R' Yechezkel Abramsky, chief rabbi of London. Rabbi Abramsky promised to exert every effort to help raise the requisite sum.

Just a few days later, Rabbi Abramsky informed Rabbi Gordon that he had found the necessary money. He had just one request to make: He, Rabbi Abramsky, would like to be the one to take the money order to the post office and mail it to the daughter's friend. He explained his reasons by relating the story of the Vilna Gaon's wife and her friend, who were collecting money for charity and who learned after the death of one of them how great a reward lies in wait even for one who waves a hand to further such a mitzvah.

If such a small thing as the wave of a hand is recorded in Heaven, Rabbi Abramsky said, then he would like to send off the check with his own two hands!

❧ A Loving Heart

Rebbetzin Chava Rivka Margolis was a guest speaker at one of the stirring Bais Yaakov conventions in the United States. Wife of Rabbi Shlomo Margolis, rabbi of the Chayei Adam congregation in Boston, she spoke eloquently of her life and of the devotion and self-sacrifice demonstrated by the righteous women of the previous generation. It is on these foundations, she stressed, that the present generation rests.

One of the women she described was her own mother, Mrs. Esther Leah Doueck, a paragon of *chesed* and of overwhelming dedication to Hashem's service.

Esther Leah's father was the prosperous R' Hirsch Sibelman, known to his fellow townsmen in Poltusk as the "Baron Hirsch." His wealth and the universal esteem in which he was held complemented one another. He wore well-tailored, expensive clothing and employed many servants. On his way to shul or to his office, everyone who passed Baron Hirsch greeted him as though he were royalty. He used his money to contribute generously to charity, to uplift paupers and support the needy.

The wheel of fortune inevitably turns. It was the outbreak of the Second World War that decreased the Baron's riches. His situation steadily worsened until all his wealth was gone and he was reduced to actual poverty. It was very difficult for him to bear his changed circumstances, but as a believing Jew he endured his pain with faith and trust in Hashem, trying to view his new situation stoically.

It was his custom to travel to see his Rebbe every *Rosh Chodesh*. On one such trip, he met a friend. They exchanged the news of their lives, and eventually came around to talking about the friend's son, who had reached the age of *shidduchim*, and Reb Hirsch's daughter, Chaya, who was in the same position. It was agreed that they would make a match. Reb Hirsch duly received his Rebbe's blessing for the union, and returned to his home.

When the friend and his son arrived at Reb Hirsch's house and began discussing the question of a dowry, it became clear that Reb Hirsch could not commit himself even to the necessary minimum for wedding expenses. The situation quickly changed: Without the money, there could be no *shidduch*.

The would-be bride, who had been eagerly looking forward to the match being finalized, was devastated to learn that finances would prevent her from marrying. She burst into bitter tears. Her older sister, Esther Leah, was witness to her pain, and it wrung her heart.

At the time Esther Leah was married to R' Avraham Doueck, a good and pious man. Grieved by the sight of her sister's anguish, she thought of the gold-and-diamond earrings she wore every Shabbos, a gift from her husband's family. She decided to sell them; her sister would be able to marry on the proceeds.

Beaming with elation, she approached her father, jewelry box in hand. "Abba, here are my earrings. I'm giving them to you with a full heart. With the money you get from selling them you can marry off Chaya."

Reb Hirsch gazed at his daughter with wonder, marveling at this act of sublime selflessness. Tears fell from his eyes even as his heart swelled with joy. The gate had now swung open for his younger daughter's nuptials. Interestingly, when R' Hirsch went to the jeweler to sell the earrings, they turned out to be worth exactly the sum he needed to cover the wedding expenses.

Esther Leah's lovingkindness knew no bounds. It was said of her that her whole heart consisted of *chesed*. Individuals in need of help turned to her as a matter of course. There were women in the Poltusk shul who were not very familiar with the *siddur*. They would find a seat beside Esther Leah, who would patiently and graciously *daven* with them. She was constantly pointing out the place for those who had lost it, and sometimes raised her voice when making the responses so that the other women would do the same. In this way, she taught the women how to *daven* without humiliating them in the slightest. Her own daughters were denied the seats nearest her, as Esther Leah was always surrounded by women begging to be allowed to pray with her.

The chaos of the World War provided ample scope for Esther Leah's kindness. One of the talents she utilized for this purpose was her fluency in several languages. At this time, many people made contact with relatives in America, asking for help in their difficult situation. For this purpose they had to write letters to be sent abroad. Esther Leah often acted as translator and, in essence, intermediary between the two sides.

Her good deeds brought their own reward. Esther Leah merited children and grandchildren who were dedicated Torah scholars, replete with *chesed*, and beloved of Heaven.

❧ True Kindness

A young girl was poised on the brink of marriage, but the union was beset by many difficulties. Rebbetzin Hinda Adler undertook to help wherever possible, but the final obstacle was — money. The bride simply had none to contribute. Finally, the Rebbetzin decided on a course of noble self-sacrifice: She sold her own jewelry to enable the young girl to be wed.

Later, when Rebbetzin Adler and her daughter were imprisoned for attempting to flee with forged documents, the nobility of her character revealed itself fully.

The Rebbetzin sensed that her end was near. The penalty for her "crime" was death. Within the next few days she would be brought before the judge, and then her sentence would be finalized. Food was scarce in prison, and the inmates were piteously hungry. Until that point, she had been permitted to receive small food packages from her family, which she had reluctantly consumed on the grounds of "Your own life takes precedence." However, in view of her conviction that she was rapidly reaching her final days, she resolved that henceforth she would distribute her food to her fellow prisoners. What was a little hunger compared to the merit of nourishing one starving Jewish soul? She happily surrendered her own bit of bread to the others, who fell on it as though it were an inestimable treasure.

Her goodness exhibited itself in the letter she managed to smuggle out to her family from her prison cell. It was not her own plight that concerned her, but that of others, the unfortunate and the sorrowful. In the letter she instructed her household to take her own dowry clothes, which were almost new, and give them to a poor bride whom she had heard was soon to marry.

✒ She Had Many Daughters

Many stories have been woven around the personality of Rebbetzin Esther Greenberg. She was unparalleled as a doer of kind deeds, a welcoming hostess, succor to the sick and a mainstay to the needy. Her home overflowed with Torah and *chesed*. A great many guests passed through her doors, and to each she gave such a welcome that he felt himself to be most important of all. A student of hers, a girl from a poor family, relates how every visit to the Rebbetzin's house made her feel as though she was the most exalted of guests. In her honor, Rebbetzin Esther would take out her best china, on which she would offer the girl the most tempting morsels in the house.

Numerous brides went to their *chupah* from Rebbetzin Esther's house. These were girls whom that good woman had raised, and whose *shidduchim* and dowries became her personal concern. She devoted her life to this project.

Once, when her own daughter was about to marry, Rebbetzin Esther took her to a certain shop to make some purchases. "Today I've brought my daughter," the Rebbetzin told the owner. "She's getting married."

In astonishment, the storekeeper replied, "Oh, really? Every week you bring a different girl here! How many daughters do you have?"

That one episode epitomizes her character. Rebbetzin Esther was indeed a mother to all those girls. The love that many felt toward her was the kind usually reserved for a mother. They behaved as though they were truly her daughters, secure in the knowledge that, in the Rebbetzin's home, they would always find solace for their troubles and a hand outstretched to comfort and assist them.

❧ A Family Value

The Chofetz Chaim's home was characterized by *chesed*. His countenance radiated love and caring for everyone he met. More than once, the members of his household witnessed his utter selflessness in sacrificing all that was precious to him for the sake of the poor.

One example among many took place on *Erev Pesach*. The Chofetz Chaim spent most of his week in the *beis midrash*, where he was accustomed to leaning on two pillows as he learned. When asked to bring home the pillowcases for washing before Pesach, it was discovered that he had not had those pillows for several months.

What had happened? It had come to his attention that good women went about the city, collecting feathers to make pillows and blankets for indigent brides. Hearing this, the Chofetz Chaim had handed over his own two pillows — and no one knew a thing about it until Pesach eve!

But it was his wife who conducted the lion's share of the *chesed* that took place in their home. Wayfarers and poor people habitually dined at her table. She was active in collecting money for needy brides and she lent assistance to those who required medical help. One of her main projects was loaning money to poor families for the purpose of establishing a business that would eventually support them.

Every Shabbos afternoon, she would leave her household and walk about town with a large sack, collecting leftover challos and bread for distribution to the poor. Once, speaking of the period when she was raising her children, the Rebbetzin mentioned that none of them ever had to see a doctor. If one of the children fell ill, the Chofetz Chaim would advise his wife to distribute a certain measure of bread to the poor. He would add his *tefillos*, and the illness would pass.

The Rebbetzin busied herself with her *chesed* projects until late at night. During the daylight hours, in addition to running her own home, she was involved in wonderful acts of kindness, lending an ear to the unfortunate and the brokenhearted. Her son, R' Leib, relates that on one visit home he found his mother rocking a baby in a cradle. To his astonishment, she told him that the child was the daughter of a fellow townsman who had been thrown into prison by the authorities. The mother was no longer living, so the Rebbetzin had taken the baby into her own home, caring for her with wondrous devotion despite her already full schedule of *chesed* and mitzvos.

After the Rebbetzin passed away, her daughter Sarah, wife of R' Tzvi Hirsch, undertook to continue all of her mother's projects. Sarah dedicated her time and energy to every poor and downtrodden individual who crossed her doorstep — with the exceptional brand of caring that she had inherited from her righteous mother.

❧ The Faithful Collector

It was not for naught that the mother of Reb Simcha Zissel of Kelm merited a son of his stature. The *Alter* of Kelm — as he came to be known — drew from her a full measure of his mother's love for Torah, and her exalted *middos* left their indelible stamp on his own character. She was as conversant in Jewish law as any *halachah* teacher. In addition, she was an active participant in many different charitable endeavors. Her primary involvement was with the sick and the poor — and each of these groups depended on continuous and generous funding.

To this end, she would make endless rounds to collect the money that was required. She took advantage of the fact that a public coach line ran through Kelm and that many of its passengers stayed at nearby inns. The Rebbetzin would stand at the inn doors as guests entered and exited, soliciting donations for her charities.

R' Mendel of Tabrig once was passing through Kelm when someone pointed out the Rebbetzin, saying that she was the daughter of R' Yisrael Salanter. He hurried over and offered her a special delicacy — cakes dipped in wine — as a sign of his respect and esteem. One of the guests, seeing the honor thus bestowed on the woman, was inspired to give her a large donation. For all her joy at the contribution to charity, she was deeply distressed by the honor bestowed on her — so distressed that she burst into tears.

Another incident reflects the Rebbetzin's strength of character. Like others involved in collecting charity in small towns, it was her custom to circulate at funerals for this purpose. On the day her only daughter died, the Rebbetzin did not alter this custom. Going around with her *tzedakah* box, she said, "Just because I am grieving and in pain, do the poor have to suffer?"

✒ If It's Difficult, It's Worthwhile

Rebbetzin Hinda Adler, daughter of the Vizhnitzer Rebbe, left behind a wealth of good deeds and inspiring acts of self-lessness. Through her tireless charitable work, she taught many the true meaning of lovingkindness.

In her youth, when only 8 or 9 years old, her father would send young Hinda out collecting money for *tzedakah*. Glowing with the joy of performing this important mitzvah, she would hasten to obey her father. As her steps echoed through the streets of Vizhnitz, her heart absorbed the messages of holiness and sacrifice for the sake of others — messages that would guide her throughout her life.

She recognized no limits and acknowledged no obstacles. Once committed to an act of charity, nothing could deter her. One example of many occurred two years before her death. Rebbetzin Adler was in London when she heard of a wedding about to take place in a prominent Chassidic family. At the time, she was involved in raising money for a certain needy family. Despite considerable hardship, she made a monumental effort to attend the wedding, in order to solicit funds for the indigent family.

A relative of the Rebbetzin's asked her whether she had been invited. When she replied in the negative, the relative was aghast. "It is not fitting for a woman of your stature and with your *yichus* to appear at a wedding in this fashion!"

Energetically, the Rebbetzin retorted, "After 120 years, how will I be able to look my holy Father in the face, when a certain family was in a difficult situation requiring enormous expenditures and I, out of foolish pride, refrained from helping?"

Rebbetzin Adler maintained fixed hours for soliciting *tzedakah* — categorically rejecting the notion that such behavior was unsuited to the dignity of an elderly woman. She was incapable of viewing such an important mitzvah as something in any way embarrassing or shameful. She would stand and collect during *Tashlich* in the 10 days between Rosh Hashanah and Yom Kippur, on *Hoshana Rabbah,* and at every opportunity that presented itself in a gathering of her fellow Jews.

But merely collecting money for the needy did not satisfy the Rebbetzin. She also urged others to become active in helping every individual in distress. So completely involved was she, and so devoted, that it became virtually impossible for her to understand why everyone else did not do as she did.

A righteous woman once came to Rebbetzin Adler with a problem: She had committed herself to raising a large sum of money for a needy family, but did not know where to find the required amount. Advised the Rebbetzin: "Do as I do. Pound the pavement for the sake of this mitzvah."

"I can't. It's very hard for me," the woman protested.

"If it's hard to do," responded the Rebbetzin wisely, "that's a sign that it's worthwhile."

🍂 The Secret Messenger

Among Sarah Schenierer's many sterling qualities was a tremendous capacity for giving. But the founder of Bais Yaakov was always careful to bestow her largess secretly, lest the recipient be insulted or humiliated.

She once heard about an individual who was in extreme need. Pesach was fast approaching, and the man was impoverished. From the moment she learned of this, Sarah Schenierer knew no peace of mind. The man's distress caused her deep personal pain. Setting aside 50 gold coins, she began to devise plans for getting the money to him. This was no easy task, as he had only recently been plunged into penury and would certainly be ashamed to accept charity.

She hit upon a plan. She visited a businessman in town who was an acquaintance of the newly poverty-stricken man. She handed him the 50 gold coins. "During *davening*, his coat will be hanging on the wall. Please slip these coins into his coat pocket while he's *davening Shemoneh Esrei*." To her delight, he agreed.

When the poor man put on his coat after the service, he found the money in his pocket. Raising his eyes to the sky, he blessed the secret messenger whom Heaven had sent to rescue him from the pit of despair.

❧ The Hidden Hand

People knew the Spinker Rebbetzin — wife of the *Chakal Yitzchak* — as a charitable woman who actively cared for others. But not many knew the true extent of her *chesed*.

It was only after she passed on that the stories began to emerge. The Jewish baker in Munkatch, R' Elimelech Hochman, related that the Rebbetzin gave him a sum of money every week to cover the cost of buying and distributing loaves of bread to poor families. Her sole condition was that they never find out who had paid.

Before her death, the Rebbetzin bade a friend to beseech the Rebbetzin's husband, the *Chakal Yitzchak*, to forgive her for sometimes taking money, without his knowledge, to give to the poor.

By the Spinker Rebbe's order, included on her tombstone were the following words: "her hands were outstretched to the poor, with bread for the hungry, and she did her charity secretly."

🎗 A Loaf of Bread

Rebbetzin Breindel Kornitzer's special qualities are recorded for posterity in the introduction of *Chiddushei R' Nechemiah,* the work written by her husband, the *Av Beis Din* of Cracow.

When the Nazi invasion of Poland precipitated the Second World War, Rebbetzin Breindel and her family fled for their lives. Fear spurred them on and they speedily covered the distance between Cracow and Lublin, where many refugees were gathered under the wing of R' Shmuel Eichenstein. Food was not provided for them, and every family had to fend for itself. One of Rebbetzin Breindel's daughters-in-law went out to search for bread. For a full night she raced through the city, seeking in vain. Only as dawn approached did she manage to lay her hand on a single loaf of bread — a single loaf to feed the entire family.

When she brought the bread home, everyone's eyes lit up. At that moment, the Rebbetzin, without a word, took the bread and quickly split it in two. In a tone that brooked no resistance, she ordered that one half of the loaf be brought upstairs to a fellow refugee, a woman with children who had no food.

Those present were amazed at this nobility of spirit, this larger-than-life generosity that enabled her to rise above her own distress and remember others even less fortunate. The Rebbetzin did not pause to contemplate what they would eat the next day; she simply shared her bread with a fellow Jew.

❧ The Silver Spoon

Two poor men arrived at the Chacham Tzvi's house. When they knocked on the door, the Chacham Tzvi's daughter answered. The household's exceptional generosity was renowned and they had come seeking a donation.

The situation had changed and the family was now in financial straits. Practically their last penny was gone. They had already given all that they could give. What to do?

Suddenly, the daughter remembered: There was still one silver spoon remaining to them. She would give it to charity. But how to divide one spoon among two paupers?

Easily. She broke the spoon into two pieces, giving the handle to one of the poor men and the bowl to the other. Happily, the two went on their way.

Witnessing this episode, the Chacham Tzvi told his daughter, "You are an *eishes chayil* — a woman of valor. You fulfilled the words, 'Her palm is open to the poor man and her hands outstretched to the pauper.'"

❧ A Mysterious Encounter

The Goldschmidt family lived in a small village near Bialystok. Bakers by profession, they worked hard to earn their meager living.

From time to time, students from the Navardok Yeshivah in Bialystok would come to meditate in solitude in the neighboring villages. The Goldschmidts' town was a special favorite. Apart from the serenity that characterized the place, it was also surrounded by a dense forest in which the yeshivah boys could be alone with their Creator and rise to new heights of spirituality.

However, though they came for spiritual purposes, the physical had to be tended to as well. All the *bachurim* knew that their meals would be supplied by R' Eliezer Goldschmidt and his wife. A burning love for Torah motivated Mrs. Goldschmidt to cook for these boys — and to send her own sons away to yeshivah at the tender age of only 9 years old!

It was during the war that her greatness fully revealed itself. As the Nazi beast sharpened its claws on European Jewry, fear gripped the tiny village. Many fled for the forests, which offered ample concealment. The Goldschmidts, however, continued to operate their bakery. "As long as there are Jews here," they said, "it is our obligation to make sure they have bread."

Then flour grew scarce, and the danger of famine arose. The villagers were hungry. One day, an elderly German officer came to Mrs. Goldschmidt, asking for bread for his soldiers. As he spoke, he held out a sack of flour. The woman busied herself at once, baking loaves all through the night. In the morning, she waited in vain for the soldiers to come fetch their bread. No one came.

At last, she ventured into the nearby army camp to inquire about the bread order. The soldiers retorted that they had not ordered any bread, nor had they any need for bread.

Surprised and puzzled, the woman returned to her village and distributed the loaves among her fellow villagers. That day, the town's Jews had bread to eat. It was a miracle.

Who was that elderly German officer?

A Torah great who heard the story gave his opinion: "It was surely Eliyahu *HaNavi*."

In return for the Goldschmidt family's willingness to sacrifice for their fellow Jews, they merited an encounter with Eliyahu *NaHavi* himself.

The Greatest Favor

This story about Sarah Schenierer, known the world over as mother of the Bais Yaakov movement, was related by a prominent writer:

One day, I entered her house to discuss something with her. It was 2 o'clock in the afternoon, and the table was set for lunch, but Sarah Schenierer had not eaten. Two women were with her, their faces bearing witness to a catastrophe. Bitterly, they poured out their story.

I went into the kitchen to wait. I found Sarah Schenierer's elderly mother there, warming up a glass of milk for her daughter. She confided that Sarah had not yet tasted a morsel that day, and expressed a wish that people would "let her daughter live," before Sarah's strength failed completely.

Apparently, these words reached Sarah Schenierer's ears. She went into the kitchen and said, "Don't worry, Mama! With Hashem's help, all will be well. They are letting me live — I *am* living, and I will continue to live even after I die. The women out there need my help. I'm going with them now, as it's getting late. I'm not hungry. Good-bye, Mama!"

Simchas Torah night, 11 p.m. I was sound asleep when my wife entered the room and told me, "Sarah Schenierer wants to talk to you." I got out of bed immediately, dressed and went into the living room. She apologized for the lateness of the hour, then proceeded to the purpose of her visit, which concerned urgent help for one of the Bais Yaakov teachers. That concluded, she turned to my wife and said, "If we wake a doctor in the middle of the night in order to save a sick person's life, do we beg his pardon? The difference is that the physician receives his payment, while the monetary value of an act of *chesed* is immeasurable. Please don't complain. Hashem will shower you with good, and the merit of the mitzvah will protect you." Wishing us a good *Yom Tov*, she took her leave.

Despite the heavy load she carried in establishing a network of Bais Yaakov schools and seminaries in Poland, Sarah Schenierer did not stay her hand when it came to the performance of *chesed*. Her days were filled with educational activity, and her nights with energetic efforts on behalf of the ill and the needy. In the wee hours of the night she would be sitting at her desk, dashing off letters to hundreds of her students — letters filled with encouragement and inspiration. Finally, as she prepared to retire, she would weigh all the day's deeds in an exacting *din v'cheshbon*.

One of the students whom she raised in her own home tells of a night when she found Sarah Schenierer lost in introspection. It was 2 a.m. The girl pleaded with Sarah to go to sleep. With a deep sigh, her teacher responded: "How can I go to sleep when I haven't done a single *chesed* for anyone all day? How can my soul ascend to the Heavenly Court empty-handed?"

The student could not bear to hear her speak this way, nor did she like the sight of Sarah sitting up so late after a full day's work, when she should be replenishing her strength with sleep. She turned to her teacher and asked, "Would you like to do a favor for someone right now?"

"I am ready and willing! Tell me quickly — who, and what?" Sarah's whole face lit up with eagerness.

The girl replied, "Do a favor for all your loyal students."

Jumping out of her seat as though prepared to dash out the door that very instant, Sarah demanded, "What? What? I'll do it with all my heart!"

"Do all your students a favor," the girl said, "all the girls to whom you will be teaching Torah and *mussar* tomorrow. Go to bed and renew your strength so that you will be able to teach with a clear head."

Sarah embraced the girl and cried, "You have given me new life!" And she immediately began reciting the bedtime *Kriyas Shema*.

❧ Open House

Welcoming guests into one's home is a mitzvah of great magnitude, especially if the visitor is ill or travel weary. Rebbetzin Raizel Abramsky specialized in this mitzvah.

Her husband, R' Yechezkel Abramsky, spent his weekdays in the Brisker *beis midrash* in Minsk, returning home in time for Shabbos. On one such occasion he told his wife that a certain Torah scholar, with whom he had learned as a young man in Telz Yeshivah, had contracted typhus. As a consequence, he said, no one would permit him to enter their home. He slept on the floor of one of Minsk's shuls, and no one would offer him a meal lest the dangerous and contagious disease spread to their families.

The moment she heard this, the Rebbetzin began making arrangements to take the sick man into her home. There he stayed for the next six months, until he had fully recovered.

During the period when R' Abramsky was serving his sentence in Siberia and the Rebbetzin stayed in their Moscow apartment, a new decree was enacted against the Jews: Anyone wishing to apply for an exit visa from the Soviet Union must reside in Moscow for at least three months. There were no hotels in Moscow at the time, nor could those desirous of leaving the Soviet Union find private rooms to rent in the capital. Many Jews turned to the Abramsky household, where they were received with open arms.

The two-and-a-half room apartment held the Abramsky family and all their various guests. The Rebbetzin allotted one room to the Rav's cousin, a woman whose children had not withstood the test of Communism and did not observe the sanctity of Shabbos or the laws of *kashrus*. The other one-and-a-half rooms held approximately 30 people! The Rebbetzin's own bed was placed in a corner, with a hanging sheet separating it from the rest of the room. People slept on the tables and under them. Every spare inch of space was turned into accommodations for one more Jew who wished to cross to the other side of the Iron Curtain.

The Rebbetzin was responsible to find food for them as well. A severe cold spell swept Russia. The only foodstuffs sold in unrationed quantities were potatoes and beets. The Rebbetzin must have carried a ton of potatoes and beets on her back that winter. Each evening, she would pick out the best of the vegetables and cook them for her guests. The Rebbetzin's quality of *chesed* was an inspiration to all who knew her.

✎ A New Lease on Life

The women of Jerusalem were exemplary for their modesty, love of simplicity, and openheartedness. Within the small crowded houses there sprouted and flourished a world steeped in love of Torah and fear of Heaven. Within these same houses a wellspring of lovingkindness and wondrous deeds impacted on the entire city.

One of these special women was Esther Rivka Blumenkrantz. Esther Rivka had a sympathetic heart, a heart that thought of *chesed* continually and sensed instinctively how others were feeling. The home that she shared with her husband, Asher Nissan, was always an open one. Numerous individuals found warmth, light and caring within those walls. New immigrants made the Blumenkrantz home their first stop. Torah scholars gathered here, along with rabbis and rebbes. Throughout the year, it was never necessary to open the door, for the door to their home was never closed.

Near their house stood a Talmud Torah. A pious but very poor man worked there for his meager living. Due to his extreme poverty he consented to wed a woman who was lame. They were married in a small and very modest ceremony. As they were standing beneath the *chupah*, the bride broke into tears at the prospect of the penury that would reign in their home.

The poor *chasan* whispered words of comfort in her ear, promising, "We'll be happy." And they were. Together they lived in harmony, if also in extreme poverty. The husband found a measure of peace and security in the Blumenkrantz house, where he was always received with joy and the offer of something hot to drink. On the days when he had to shop in the market, he would borrow Esther Rivka's shopping bag and return it faithfully the next day. This went on for some time.

One day, however, the man borrowed the bag but, for the first time, did not return it the following day. Esther Rivka's sixth sense told her that something was wrong. She decided to pay a visit to the man's home to investigate.

Arriving at the tiny apartment, she found the couple inside, woebegone. Despair radiated from both their faces, reflecting the misery they were feeling. Relatives from abroad had come to Jerusalem, and had invited the entire extended family on a pleasure trip — all except for this couple, with the excuse that they would find the journey too difficult. Both husband and wife were depressed and discouraged, feeling as if no one in the world needed them or considered them important. So broken in spirit were they that they could not muster up the spirit to step out of their own home.

Esther Rivka's unexpected entrance effected an instant and amazing transformation. New life flowed into the poor couple as they saw the depths of her concern for them. Someone really did think about them; someone did care about them. They had something to hold onto in the dark world in which they felt themselves plunged.

From that moment, the mood of the pair changed from anguish to joy. They felt reborn. That good and caring woman, Esther Rivka Blumenkrantz, had given two Jewish souls a new lease on life!

❧ Simple Hospitality

One of the finest homes of the previous generations was that of R' Chaikin of the yeshivah at Aix-les-Bains in France. *Chesed* flowed from the very walls of the Chaikin house. Numerous guests made it their headquarters, and families in need of a roof over their heads found welcome shelter and aid there. Most of the good work was done by Rebbetzin Fraidel Chaikin, who burned with a mission to help others, at the personal cost of hours of sleep, money and strength.

On many occasions, the household included total strangers whose origins or destinations were unknown. They came for a meal and a bed. Once, the guests included a woman and her four children. The Rebbetzin explained to anyone who asked that the woman's husband had remained in Morocco, trying to wind up his affairs before coming to join his family. In the interim, the mother and children had no place to sleep. In the natural course of things, they had found their way to shelter and warmth — at the Chaikin house. On another occasion, an entire family spent several months at the Chaikins en route from Morocco to a new home in France.

The Rebbetzin always greeted her guests with great joy and a hand outstretched in genuine welcome. Once, she took several children in for an extended period of time, as their mother could not adequately cope with them. The grateful mother bought a present for the Rebbetzin: the *Tzenah U'Re'enah*. Seeing it, the Rebbetzin burst into tears. "Why a present? Why did you do that?" She performed her acts of lovingkindness out of pure love, without any thought of receiving recompense or reward.

Yom Kippur found many of the town's residents coming to *daven* at the yeshivah. What to do with the children? It was understood that the children were to be left at the *Rosh Yeshivah's* house until the stars were twinkling in the sky at the end of the fast. When the parents came to collect their offspring, the Rebbetzin had tea and cake waiting for them. When they offered to help, she replied, "No, no — you're weak from the fast."

The Chaikins hosted a *Sheva Berachos* meal for every resident and yeshivah student who married. This was no easy feat. It entailed cooking, baking and preparing all the meal's delicacies, as well as washing all the dishes and cleaning the house afterward. But no one ever heard the Rebbetzin complain that the work was too hard. She always performed it with joy.

Her husband, the *Rosh Yeshivah,* would quote the words, "And the poor shall be members of your household." In other words, it is best to deal with guests in simplicity, as though they were members of the household — otherwise, one might be tempted not to host guests at all. He held to this course with reference to all their many guests and to the hundreds of *Sheva Berachos* feasts that took place in his home. It was better to do it simply than not to be able to do it at all.

Students at the yeshivah attest to the fact that there was no lock on the *Rosh Yeshivah's* door. Everyone knew that he could walk into that great man's home at any time to obtain what he needed. *Chesed* flowed from the walls — directly into the hearts of all who stepped through that door.

‌ A Life of Giving

Mrs. Chaya Schechter's home in Tel Aviv was reminiscent of the tent of Avraham *Avinu*. Countless visitors passed through her door and received what they needed — and more. Not a day passed without its share of guests. Great men of Torah dined at her table, as did simpler folk as well. She and her husband treated each guest as though he were a king. It was not uncommon for visitors — sometimes large groups of 10 to 30 people — to extend their stay for months at a time. Everyone felt at home there. They felt wanted and respected.

Once, a young family consisting of three small children and their ailing mother stayed with the Schechters. Mrs. Schechter tended personally and devotedly to the young woman's every need. With great maternal caring she made sure that the mother had the best food to eat and that she got sufficient rest. Needless to say, she also took it upon herself to care for the children. After an extended period of time, the mother finally recovered her health and her strength and wished to return to her own home. When she and her children went to take their leave of Mrs. Schechter, they were astounded at her reaction. "Why are you rushing away so soon?" She truly found it difficult to part from her guests.

The wife of a certain rebbe relates that one night during Israel's War of Independence, with Jerusalem under attack, her family fled under cover of darkness to Tel Aviv. Arriving in that city, they had no idea where to turn next. Then, remembering the Schechters, they headed in that direction. The large family arrived at the Schechter house in the middle of the night — to be welcomed with warmth and joy. To free up some beds, Mrs. Schechter moved several of her children from their beds and set down mattresses for them on the floor. When the Rebbetzin saw this, she protested, "Please, let them sleep, we'll use the mattresses." Mrs. Schechter responded: "They've already slept enough, now they can help others."

The desire to give to others was present in her even as a young child. It was a time when there was no work to be had, and where there is no livelihood there is no bread in the house. In innocence, the little girl went to her parents and said, "I'm such a hard worker. You can sell me as a servant for a good price and then the whole family will have food to eat. When things get better you can buy me back."

Her son has this to add about his exemplary mother. Once, she sent him to a neighbor's house to borrow a sum of money. When he returned with the money, she set the envelope aside and left it, untouched. The boy questioned why she asked to borrow money if she was not going to use it. Mrs. Schechter explained to her son that she did it so that the neighbors would feel comfortable coming to *them* for a loan in their own time of need!

✿ Boulissa's Dedication

Difficult times had fallen on Jerusalem. Typhus raged in the city, claiming many victims. R' Ezra Attia's home was not spared: His mother, Leah, fell ill with the dread disease. Reb Ezra was living in Egypt at the time, having fled there to escape the military draft then in effect in Palestine. His wife, Boulissa, had remained behind in Israel. It was she who cared for her mother-in-law, visiting her faithfully every day, feeding her and devoting herself to the older woman's every need despite the heavy burdens she already carried.

Poverty and scarcity were their lot, as Jerusalem was cut off from its supply lines. Rebbetzin Boulissa and her brother,

R' Natan Salim, stood in line at the *shuk*, sometimes for a full day, to sell their household goods for a little money with which to purchase food for their family.

The good woman managed to find an additional source of income: carrying buckets of water from a well several kilometers away, which she would sell at the homes of the wealthy. The labor was backbreaking but it was the only means she could find to keep her family and her mother-in-law alive.

The typhus epidemic strengthened its hold on the city. Many of the sick were abandoned by relatives fearful of contracting the disease, but Rebbetzin Attia had no such qualms. She continued to visit and feed her mother-in-law and others, in the devout belief that messengers of a mitzvah do not come to harm. With superhuman strength and dedication, she brought many back from death's door — and many individuals owe their lives to her.

Part Nine:
Righteous Women

❧ An Eye on the Next world

I N HIS INTRODUCTION TO HIS FATHER'S CLASSIC commentaries to *Shulchan Aruch, Derishah* and *Perishah,* R' Yospah Falk writes in praise of his father, the author. Near the end of the introduction, he turns the spotlight of his praise on his mother: "She...is the one who has brought all this honor to my father and teacher. She has crowned her husband, helping him and his students to involve themselves in Torah."

He continues: His mother's light reflects not only onto their own family, but onto the entire generation. "She was the glory of Jewish women, guiding them on the right path. Therefore, she deserves to be honored and to have several of her good deeds recorded in this work, to be remembered down through the generations, so that all Jewish daughters may learn from her example."

As the only daughter of a wealthy man, she had the capacity to indulge in her every desire. But she refrained from doing so, turning away from worldly pleasures and choosing instead to guarantee herself a portion in the World to Come.

Not only did she avoid pleasure in this world; she also afflicted herself with fasting. After her husband passed away, the widow spent the next 17 years in daily fasting. At night, she would not touch anything that was derived from any living creature or from fruit trees, eating only enough to sustain life. In honor of the Shabbos she would prepare various delicacies of which she partook very little, sending the rest to her relatives and to the poor. All her life, winter or summer, she would rise hours before the sun was up, to immerse herself in prayer. She possessed a key to the women's section at the shul, and was always first to arrive and last to leave: It was at least an hour or two after everyone else had gone that she completed her own devotions.

After *davening*, she would not involve herself in the mundane, concentrating instead on studying the weekly Torah portion with Rashi and other commentaries. As her son attests — and as all of her husband's students knew firsthand — when Torah matters were discussed at their table she held her own, occasionally offering an original interpretation, sweet as honey, particularly about the laws pertaining to women. She was nearly as knowledgeable as renowned teachers of Torah.

The widow had a yearning to live in *Eretz Yisrael*, and she managed to actualize that dream, settling in Jerusalem for her last eight years. Because of her fasting and self-affliction, she lived only 58 years. When her soul departed this world her memory was greatly honored, and she was buried with vast respect four cubits from the grave of Zechariah *HaNavi*.

The son concludes: "May her merit stand in good stead for us, for our children, and for the entire House of Israel — Amen, may it be Your Will!"

✒ Just Like the Matriarchs

R' Avraham HaLevi Horowitz was also known as the Shelah HaKadosh, after his great work, *Shnei Luchos HaBris*. His son wrote the *Vavei HaAmudim*, found at the end of his father's work. There he heaps praise upon the Shelah HaKadosh for supporting Torah all his life and for feeding 80 guests at his table on Shabbos and *Yom Tov*.

Behind that *tzaddik* stood the righteous Rebbetzin, about whom the son writes: "Everyone who knew her will testify that she did not depart from any of our Matriarchs' holy ways …Her hand was always out to help my father, who spent all the money his wife had brought with her from her father's house in support of Torah scholars. Not only did she not look askance on this practice, but she added to it on her own …Look around, and see whether you can find a better woman in all these things — one who rejected the mundane and did everything for the sake of the next world."

He concludes, "And it is because of her that Hashem blessed my father, so that he merited so much honor and glory."

✒ Ode to a Mother

In his introduction to the Maharsham's *Da'as Torah*, R' Sholom Schwadron writes about his own mother, who died in Jerusalem in the year 5722 (1962):

"Rashi, in his commentary on *Mishlei* (30:17), explains the words '*likhas em*' as referring to the creases and wrinkles that appear on a mother's face. When we look at the wrinkles that have gathered on our mother's face over the 42 years of her widowhood (she was 35, the mother of six young children when lost her husband), we are seized with a trembling awe and respect at her strength and endurance. She lost her captain and her sailor at one blow, and there was none to help her. Each day she had to struggle to provide for her family, to feed them, to dress them, to support and help them, and to educate them in Torah and fear of Heaven. But she did not stumble beneath this heavy load. Her feet did not falter nor her hands weaken. She went her way with courage and strength, step after step, with faith in *Hashem Yisbarach* — the Father of orphans and Judge of widows!

"In addition to all of this, her brother — poor and sickly, suffering both physically and mentally — lived in her home. She tended to him and cared for his needs with devotion and faithfulness, as though he were one of her own children.

"We saw the meaning of true *chesed*, of simplicity, of humility, of natural purity. She would reach out a hand to help the stumbler, and indeed behaved in this fashion in everything she did ...

"Above and beyond all this, we must stand in wonder at the level of her Torah knowledge, which was extraordinary for a woman even in the generations preceding hers. Hashem graced her with mighty talents, and she, with remarkable diligence, rose higher and higher. It seems incredible to relate that every day, after hours of hard work — physical work that entailed lifting and running about, climbing many flights of stairs in homes and courtyards, selling bread, butter, etc., to make life easier for her father-in-law and to support her own children — and then performing the housework, cooking, cleaning, feeding the children, etc., she would use the few moments that remained for herself to enter a new world: the world of reading, studying and learning. She found solace for all her troubles in the books that rested on her table, drawing from them comfort and encouragement for her spirit. In them she found light to illuminate the darkness of her widow's life — because she was a great, wise and educated woman!

"It was wondrous, too, to watch her pour out her heart in prayer to Hashem morning and night, in a yearning tone that pierced the heart. When she pleaded with her Maker in the words of King David, the rhythm of every syllable punctuated by the tears that dripped onto the pages of her *Tehillim* — then we knew what it was her soul longed for... And it comes as no surprise, for she understood the significance of the words she murmured, and rose with them to heights of purity.

"Believe this if you wish (and the stubborn may choose not to believe); it's all the same to us. But we know this, too: Every week, she would learn the Torah portion with Rashi's commentary, and sometimes with other commentaries such as the *Ramban*, the *Ohr HaChaim* and the *Kli Yakar*, and she was able to grasp them and discuss their difficulties and resolutions like a rabbi. Similarly, she had a broad knowledge of *Tanach*, which she reviewed many times. She even attempted the Oral Torah.

"Once, in a conversation, she mentioned several tractates that she had learned by herself (this was during my father's lifetime, when she was not so burdened). We would see her sitting at night with a copy of *Ein Yaakov* and other collections of *Aggados Shas*; she would return to the beginning and review them several times. In fact, it would be no exaggeration to say that in the area of *aggadah* she was more conversant than a number of men who call themselves Torah scholars!

"Indeed, she deserves the names we called her in our opening words: noble in her endurance, noble in Torah and mitzvos, and patient in her suffering. 'Praiseworthy is the people for whom this is so, praiseworthy is the people whose G-d is Hashem.'"

❧ Who Is a Good Wife?

R' Yosef, the Rav of Posen, was married to the daughter of R' Yechezkel Landau, the author of the *Noda B'Yehudah*. All through their married life, the Rebbetzin would enter a room where he was talking with other men and mock him to their faces, declaring that he was an empty man without a single positive character trait. R' Yosef would listen to this scorn without saying a word, never once scolding or berating her for this behavior.

The people of Posen were amazed. Why was the Rebbetzin acting this way toward her righteous husband, when even her own father had treated him with great — indeed, extraordinary — respect and affection, referring to him as "all my *nachas* in my old age; in Torah and in deeds he is singular in his generation."

At first the townspeople could not bear this insult to their Rabbi. With time, however, they gradually grew accustomed to it, though they were still deeply distressed that the Rebbetzin did not know how to honor her husband. It was only after R' Yosef departed this world, in Adar of 5561 (1801), that the mystery was solved.

As their departed Rabbi lay before them, with everyone weeping over him, the Rebbetzin entered, also weeping. In a loud voice, she cried, "R' Yosef, R' Yosef! Acknowledge for all to see that *you* were the one who forced me to ridicule you in public all your life! I did not do it from an evil heart, Heaven forbid, or because I did not know how to appreciate your greatness in Torah and piety. I did it because it was your will, because before we married you made a condition that I treat you frivolously and mockingly in front of others so that you would not fall into the trap of arrogance. Even as a young boy everyone was calling you a complete *tzaddik*. You were afraid that pride and arrogance would cause you to lose your place in the next world. Against my will, I did what you charged me to do. Who is a good wife? One who fulfills her husband's will. Who knows better than I how great was your righteousness?"

Suddenly, the onlookers saw the dead man's head nodding in agreement.

❧ The Day the Clocks Stopped

In his eulogy for his wife, Rebbetzin Miriam, Rabbi Yaakov Neiman, *Rosh Yeshivah* of Yeshivas Ohr Yisrael in Petach Tikvah, said as follows: "On the morning of the day she died, I rose from my bed, glanced at the clock and saw that it had stopped running. I went to look at a different clock — but it, too, had stopped at the same hour as the first. Suspecting nothing, I hurried to the yeshivah for *Shacharis*. It was in the middle of the *tefillah* that they brought me the terrible news. According to the doctor, it turned out that, precisely at the moment of her death, all the clocks had stopped."

He added, "They tell a story about the *gaon*, R' Yitzchak Elchanan Spector, *av beis din* of Kovno. Before he left this world, he said that there were two things he would be happy to bring before *HaKadosh Baruch Hu*. The first was the fact that he arranged kosher food for Jewish soldiers. The second was that he had suffered from asthma. I, too, say that my wife will bring two things before *HaKadosh Baruch Hu*. The first is that she did not wish to remain in the Diaspora and made every effort to come here, to our Holy Land, where she accepted every difficulty with love. And she also suffered terribly from asthma. There is no doubt, therefore, that she has merited a place in *Gan Eden* alongside the other righteous women."

Part Ten:

Love of Torah

❧ Two Diamonds

YESHIVAH OHEL TORAH OF BARANOVICH WAS PLUNGED into financial difficulty, and the situation was growing worse with each passing month. The problem reached the point where it was becoming impossible to pay for food for the *bachurim*. The *Rosh Yeshivah*, the *gaon* R' Elchonon Wasserman, decided to personally knock on philanthropists' doors to ask for help in keeping the yeshivah open.

There was hardly any question about where to begin. The name "Davis" had become synonymous with succor for Lithuanian yeshivahs' financial troubles. From every corner of the land came requests for help, and he was known to receive one and all pleasantly and respectfully. He resided in a beautiful villa in nearby Minsk, which he had turned into a headquarters for many charitable activities.

A glimpse of the large, lavishly decorated villa struck awe into all who saw it. The stairs were made of green marble; the knobs of the banisters were solid gold. The outer staircase curved gracefully down from the front door, adorning the outside of the house like the finest furnishing. The villa itself was comprised of several stories, topped by a red roof shaded by the tall trees that grew stately on the lawn. What the inside of the house looked like only his guests knew. They told of luxuriant rugs that covered the length of the floors, of expensive chandeliers and costly sofas — all testimony to the owner's vast wealth.

To this house came a steady stream of visitors: on the one hand, businessmen and merchants to transact business and, on the other, individuals coming to solicit his assistance in their time of need. At the head of this second group were the *Roshei Yeshivah* and Torah greats who visited his home from time to time to engage his help in supporting Torah in their institutions. One of these, as we have noted, was Reb Elchonon, now making his way to the Davis house.

It was a bitter day, cold and snowy. The roads were difficult to traverse and the normal routes were closed. The only way to get anywhere was on foot. Reb Elchonon paid no attention to the difficulties: He was engaged in the mitzvah of supporting a yeshivah, which he regarded as tantamount to saving all of *Klal Yisrael.*

The further he went, the harder it snowed. Doggedly, Reb Elchonon walked on. At one point, he paused for a moment to look down at himself. He saw all the mud and snow that had accumulated on his coat and boots and wondered how he could enter the rich man's house in such a condition. It would be very unpleasant to visit such a beautiful home looking like this: His boots would soil the expensive furnishings.

Then he remembered a detail he had noticed on a previous visit to the Davis house. There was a side door leading to the kitchen, used by the tradesmen delivering food supplies and milk. There were no rugs in that area and he would not ruin anything. That, he decided, was where he would enter.

In the villa's kitchen, the two Davis daughters were busy preparing lunch. To their surprise, they heard an unexpected knock at the tradesman's door. They went to the window to see who was there — the egg man, perhaps, or the one who came around selling cheese. Instead, through the window they spied a very distinguished figure. Quickly, they opened the door — and recognized the *Rosh Yeshivah's* familiar face. In great excitement they ran to their father. "Father, Father, Reb Elchonon is here!"

"Reb Elchonon?" their father asked in astonishment. "Where? I didn't see him come in."

"Here, in the kitchen!"

Mr. Davis entered the kitchen and saw Reb Elchonon standing in the doorway, reluctant to go any further and apologizing for the dirtied state that had led him to choose the side door. Suddenly, Mr. Davis broke into bitter tears. He wept and wept, and as the tears streamed down his face he managed to utter a few words. "What have you done to me, Rebbe?"

Reb Elchonon gazed at him, not understanding the reason for the tears. In a choked voice, the rich man asked, "Rebbe, how have I sinned? Where have I gone wrong? Why is the *Rosh Yeshivah* doing this to me?"

For a moment, thinking that someone may have been gossiping about him, Reb Elchonon asked, "What have I done to you? I don't know of any evil I have done to you. On the contrary, we have always been on friendly terms."

When he had controlled himself enough to speak, Mr. Davis said, "Rebbe, you have ruined my daughter's upbringing! All day my daughters see a house filled with silver and gold, money and more money, merchants buying and selling. This is what accompanies them day in and day out. I am always afraid: Why would my daughters wish to marry *bnei Torah*? All they will want is money! But I've comforted myself with the thought that they know one thing: They know that the Torah is worth more in my eyes than money. When the time comes for my *shiur*, I leave everything and go learn, even if the house is full of men who have come on business. To me, learning is sacred.

"But now, what has the *Rosh Yeshivah* done, calling me to come into the kitchen instead of entering through the living room? Is this what he is showing my girls, that it is impossible for him to enter through the front door with mud and snow on his boots? Where is *kavod haTorah*? What will they think now — that rugs are worth more than Torah or the honor due to a *Rosh Yeshivah*?" He buried his face in his hands and wept more bitterly than before.

"I understand," Reb Elchonon said. "But what will you have me do now? See how I look."

"I wish to request a favor: that the *Rosh Yeshivah* will come with me through the front door, that he will walk on the rugs and sit on the sofas. Let them be ruined — by all means! Let my daughters see, and take the message into their hearts — that the Torah and the *Rosh Yeshivah* are more important than rugs and furniture."

Later, when recounting the story, Reb Elchonon said, "I had no choice. I went around to the front door, dirtying the house with my mud, because he would not leave me in peace until I did as he wished."

And he went on to add that the philanthropist's reward for raising his daughters the way he did earned him two diamonds: R' Avraham Yitzchak Bloch and his brother. Both disseminated Torah, one as the Rosh Yeshivah of Telz, and the other as a lecturer in that yeshivah. At their sides were those two outstanding women of valor, Mr. Davis' daughters, brimming with a love of Torah that they had absorbed in their father's house.

Later, when the Communists took over the country, all of Mr. Davis' wealth was confiscated and he became a very poor man. But he found solace in saying, "Nothing of all my wealth is left except my two diamonds — my two sons-in-law."

❧ Four Requests

The Sfas Emes's daughter-in-law, Chaya, wife of R' Moshe Bezalel, was descended from an illustrious lineage. When she passed away, she left a will that demonstrated a remarkably lofty level of love for Torah and nurture of her husband's Torah study.

The will contained four instructions. The first was to light a specific pair of candles near her body. There was no electricity in those days, and her husband would learn at night by candlelight. Every morning, Chaya would gather up the remaining drops of wax, from which, over the years, she fashioned two large candles. These were the candles she ordered lit near her body.

Her second order was that her body be carried out by way of the room where her husband did his learning.

Then she instructed the shroud makers to make her shroud out of a shirt belonging to the author of the *Chiddushei HaRim*, which she had received as an inheritance.

When she and R' Moshe Bezalel were newly married, his father, the Sfas Emes, wrote a letter to her grandfather, R' Naftali Ungar, asking for help in supporting R' Moshe Bezalel and his wife, Chaya. He added, "I am not writing this for the sake of my son, R' Moshe Bezalel, but rather for the sake of your righteous granddaughter..." and he went on to heap praises on his daughter-in-law.

The fourth thing Chaya ordered in her will was that this letter be placed in her grave.

🙊 With Her Own Hands

There is love of Torah, and there is self-sacrifice for the Torah's sake. Above and beyond all this is the diligent desire to support Torah study. For a woman, this means rising to every challenge and physically assisting her husband in every possible way. This was the level reached by Rebbetzin Elyashiv. Indeed, she stands as a symbol that epitomizes this approach.

Every night, when the Rav would rise to begin his learning, the Rebbetzin would get up as well, and prepare him a cup of hot coffee. This was no small matter. In earlier times water had to be heated in a special pot on a paraffin stove, involving considerable bother. But what was a little bother compared to the incredible privilege of helping her learned husband? She rose in joy every night to prepare him his hot drink.

In her old age, one of her daughters bought the Rebbetzin an electric teapot which would heat water at the press of a button. There was no longer any need for her to get up at night; the Rav could easily heat the water himself. The Rebbetzin refused the gift vehemently. "Will they take this mitzvah away from me, too?" she protested.

With her own hands, she would wash her husband's clothes, taking great care that they should never appear stained. Even when her children took the rest of the laundry to their house for washing, she insisted on washing the Rav's clothes herself. This was another mitzvah from which she adamantly refused to be parted.

✒ Sweet Music

The *gaon*, R' Yosef Shlomo Kahaneman, the Ponovizher Rav, told of a righteous woman who lived in the city of Ponovizh, in Lithuania. One day, he spied her walking back and forth in front of the *beis midrash*.

"Would you like me to call your husband out of the *beis midrash* for you?" he asked.

"No," she replied. "I am simply enjoying listening to the sound of his Torah."

The Rav concluded, "That woman merited seeing her husband become great in Torah, with many students, and having children of her own who were outstanding Torah scholars."

When R' Avraham Wolf told this story, he would add: "'*Rabbos banos asu chayil v'at alis al kulanah.*' Other women have done much to support Torah, but this woman rose above the others, for love of Torah as a value is the absolute basis for building a Torah home."

✒ A Widow Worries

Rabbi Sholom Schwadron related the following:

My mother was a *tzaddekes*. But she was also very poor. As a widow, she supported herself and her children by selling bread. Day after day she would circulate among the houses with her loaves for sale.

I remember once, in later years, finding her in bed, crying. "What will I bring with me to the next world? Shalom'ke, what will I bring to the next world?"

I answered, "Ima, you used to sell bread. How many loaves did you sell in one day — a hundred? How many stairs did you climb each day? Five or six hundred? How many years did you do this? So-and-so many years. In that case, don't worry. You did all this to feed your children, so that they could learn Torah. If they weigh all that bread and count all the stairs you went up and down all those years, they will surely decree in your favor!"

My mother answered, "You've given me life, my son. You have given me life!"

✍ A Special Occasion

Not every day do we go out and buy a new dress — and this was certainly the case a hundred years ago. A new dress was an event, a celebration. In the home where the *gaon*, R' Yitzchak Hutner, author of the *Pachad Yitzchak*, was raised, his mother came to his father one day and asked, "Since I have a new dress, when shall I start wearing it for the first time — on Shabbos, *Yom Tov*, or some other day?"

Her husband, wishing both to make her a part of her son's learning and to inculcate in the boy a love of Torah, answered, "Next week, Yitzchak will be finishing *Maseches Bava Kamma*. Wear the new dress at the *siyum*."

Joyously, she turned to her son and said, "My dear, I will wear the new dress at your *siyum* next week!"

Yitzchak looked at his mother and saw the deep, genuine happiness that the decision had brought her and the warm tears that fell on the page of his open Gemara, leaving a profound and lasting impression on the young boy's heart.

❧ I Owe Her My Life!

Among the old stones of the Jerusalem houses walked a man wearing the uniform of the Polish army. This unusual sight aroused much curiosity among the residents, who peeked at him from their windows, wondering who he was. On one street, he stopped to ask a passerby, in Yiddish, where Rabbi Benzion Bruck lived.

The man stared at him in astonishment. "Why are you looking for that *gaon?*"

The soldier answered, "He was my *Rosh Yeshivah* in Greiba."

The Jerusalemite directed him to a house that everyone in the area knew well: R' Benzion's home.

The man walked up to the house and knocked at the door. He was invited to enter. As he did, he introduced himself. The *Rosh Yeshivah* shook his hand warmly, and asked why the man was dressed as a Polish soldier. The man explained that Poland still maintained a draft, and with the outbreak of the war he had been forced to join a unit being formed in England to fight the Germans. Now en route from England via the Suez Canal, they were passing through Palestine.

The soldier apologized for the necessarily short visit, as he had to rejoin his unit shortly. The military police dealt harshly with potential deserters. Anyone who did not carry out an order was severely punished, and anyone caught trying to desert was summarily shot. The soldier spoke a while with the *Rosh Yeshivah,* accepted his words of encouragement and prepared to return to his camp.

Suddenly, Rebbetzin Leah, the *Rosh Yeshivah's* wife, stood up and said forcefully, "No! You are not going to stay on with the Polish army. It's bad for you, for your *Yiddishkeit.* You are staying here!"

"B-but this is a matter of life and death," the soldier stammered.

"I will not let you return to the Polish army. You can become contaminated there." As she spoke, she gathered up several garments suitable for a yeshivah student, thrust them at the soldier and urged him to switch his uniform for them.

The soldier, knowing the grave risk, hesitated. Seeing this, those neighbors who were present urged the Rebbetzin not to endanger his life by causing him to desert. But she stood firm. The soldier left the room. When he returned moments later, he was clad in every detail as a yeshivah *bachur*.

The Rebbetzin directed him to the shul where her husband's yeshivah was located. Without another word she took the uniform into the yard, prepared a bonfire and threw it into the flames.

She stood by the fire until every last shred was consumed. Only the metal Polish emblem remained, a symbol of her own courage — the courage of a Jewish mother anxious for a Jewish son.

Just hours later, Polish soldiers fanned out to seek the deserter who had left camp and never returned. They instituted a house-to-house search, giving rise to widespread fear and apprehension. But Hashem arranged matters so that, the very next morning, urgent orders arrived dispatching that unit to Europe. They went at once, leaving everything behind — including the missing soldier.

During the course of the war, every last soldier from that unit was killed in battle. Only one remained alive: the young R' Aryeh Yigdal, in Jerusalem. For all his remaining years he would say with gratitude, "I owe my entire life to Rebbetzin Leah Bruck!"

✿ Open House

The Shinelson family lived in the same building as Kollel Chazon Ish in Bnei Brak. Their first-floor apartment was tantamount to public property, with the door open to *kollel* members at all hours of the day and night. Anyone might wander into the kitchen to take a drink of cold water from the steady supply that was kept on hand in the refrigerator. There was always a bed available for those who needed to rest. The Shinelson home was a place where love of Torah was matched by love of *chesed*. For this family, welcoming these Torah scholars and caring for their needs was its own unique mission in this world.

The brunt of that mission, naturally, was borne by Chaya Rivka Shinelson. From the moment she married, she undertook to glorify the Torah to the fullest extent of her abilities. She was an educated woman, well versed in a variety of subjects and fluent in several languages. In the depths of her being, however, she recognized that her goal in this world must be to build an edifice for the next. Accordingly, immediately after the wedding the couple settled in a modest apartment in Bnei Brak planning to establish a home dedicated solely to Torah. They developed a close relationship with the Chazon Ish's wife, and Rabbi Shinelson numbered among the first 10 men to learn in the *kollel*.

Chaya Rivka Shinelson knew no greater love than her love of the Torah life. Her entire ambition was focused on the perfect fulfillment of Hashem's commandments. Her greatest joy came from performing these mitzvos and serving those who had dedicated their lives to Torah. This was the reason behind the open-door policy she maintained from early in the morning until very late at night — all for *bnei Torah*. Once, when asked whether the sound of voices raised in learning from the *beis midrash* above disturbed her, she replied, "Not only does it not disturb me, on the contrary — those voices lift my heart and make my sleep more pleasant!"

Early each day, she would ask the members of her household to rise and dress quickly, so that the apartment could be opened to the public. Many visitors slept there for months on end, living with the Shinelsons as though with their own families. They might be new immigrants who had not yet arranged for a place to live, or individuals facing difficult circumstances of one kind or another. All came to this household and found what they needed. It was understood that the traditional *kiddush* on Rosh Hashanah and during the *hakafos* on Simchas Torah was always held in the Shinelson apartment.

In her ardent longing for the life of the World to Come, Rebbetzin Shinelson spared hardly a thought for the concerns of this world. So great was her joy in Torah that she had none left over for material matters. Her family attests that, in all the long years of her marriage — nearly 50 of them — she bought only three new dresses, on the occasion of her children's weddings. The rest of the time she managed with what she had, cleanly and with dignity, but also with simplicity. She was never troubled by a lack of *things*. Her satisfaction at supporting Torah revealed itself in her countenance, which habitually radiated happiness and contentment.

The four walls of her home can testify to this remarkable woman's love of Torah — a love that expressed itself in everyday acts of caring, and a total devotion to those who learn our holy Torah.

Part Eleven:
Brides and Grooms

❧ The Steadfast Groom

I T WAS ONLY NATURAL THAT THE DAUGHTER OF THE prosperous Reb Shmuel Shmelka Reich would marry an outstanding young man. Day after day, matchmakers visited the opulent Reich home in Prague to recommend the "best boy in the world" for this special girl.

An only child, Perel incorporated every fine quality that might be sought in a *bas Yisrael*. Whoever married her would be privileged to a life of both Torah and prosperity. As yet, however, despite all the suggestions, Perel had not found her destined husband.

One day, a childhood friend of Reb Shmelka's came to visit. His host treated him with great respect, inviting him in and asking him to sit down. The two sat opposite each other, chatting about this and that, until the guest revealed his purpose in coming.

"I live in Posen, which also happens to be the home of a very respected family. The father, Reb Bezalel, has four sons. Each one of them has an excellent character, and they have all won names for themselves as outstanding Torah scholars with brilliant futures ahead of them. The oldest three have married into fine families, but the youngest son, Leib, has just reached marriageable age. I thought it would be suitable for him to enter your honored family, and for you to have such a young man as your son-in-law. This is the boy you've been *davening* for."

Reb Shmelka was persuaded by these words to travel to Posen to meet the young man in question. From the moment the two met, Leib found favor in Reb Shmelka's eyes. Matters proceeded at a rapid pace, until both sides announced with joy that the young *illui*, Leib, had become engaged to Perel. The happy news spread quickly.

Within days, however, dark clouds began to gather in the Prague skies. It was a troubled time, as Christian hatred for the Jews periodically erupted into violent action. One night, terrible cries woke the Jews from their sleep. The glare of flickering flames lit the entire city. A raging fire devoured one house after another, until it reached the Jewish quarter. Many homes in this part of town were rapidly demolished as well. One of these belonged to Reb Shmelka Reich. His beautiful house was reduced to ashes and rubble.

As if that were not trouble enough, the Christians then accused the Jews of starting the fire, and fresh violence erupted in the Jewish quarter. Jews were beaten mercilessly — Reb Shmelka among them. For many days he lay comatose in his bed; he had been struck down twice: His wealth was gone and his body was broken.

Gradually Reb Shmelka began to recover from his wounds. As he slowly healed, his thoughts turned to his daughter's nuptials. In an agony of spirit he recalled his promise to his future son-in-law to provide the financial security Leib would need to involve himself in Torah to the exclusion of all else.

Now his dearest hopes had been swallowed up in poverty and anguish. He would have to inform Leib of the change in his fortunes.

Naturally, these concerns were shared by his family. The spirit of the entire household would have been depressed in the extreme, if not for the valiant Perel.

"Father," she said, "I understand the situation. We can't fulfill our promises to Leib. He has a great future ahead of him and needs a family that is able to support him. If it is impossible for us to do so, we must send him a letter saying that, for our part, we are prepared to break the *shidduch* and release him from his obligation to us."

Inwardly, Perel wondered whether she had been found unworthy of such a groom. Had all this evil befallen her family on her account? In tears, she beseeched her Creator, "I cannot bear the shame. Have pity on Your daughter, Perel *bas* Shmuel." She could only cling to the tenuous hope that something would happen at the 11th hour to save the day.

The letter made its way to Posen, where word of the tragic events in Prague had already preceded it. R' Leib read the letter, then sat down at once to reply.

"Why break the *shidduch*? There is no reason to do so ... We must continue to be strong in our faith, for good days will certainly return."

The euphoria with which this letter was received can well be imagined. Every line bespoke the young man's fine character and steadfast faith. It was a missive to comfort the heaviest heart, and it brought great encouragement to the family.

Reb Shmelka's family moved into a meager hut, where cold was rampant and darkness seemed to swallow the light. Their lives were very difficult to bear, especially in contrast to the memory of the splendors lost to them. Poverty and pain brought the family to a very low point. The father was still recovering from his injuries, the wife was tending to his needs — and where was their livelihood to come from?

Once again, Perel rose to the occasion. "Enough of this

insufferable situation! I'm going to do something to help. I can support us by baking bread. I'll go out to the marketplace every day to sell my loaves, and we'll get by on that."

If not for the hunger that oppressed every member of the household, Perel's suggestion would have been rejected out of hand. As it was, she rose early each morning, baked her loaves of bread and went out to peddle them from a modest stall in the marketplace. She did not bring home a great deal of money, but it was enough for them to live on.

One day, as she stood at her stall, a soldier cantered up on his horse. Unsheathing his sword, he thrust the point into a loaf and whisked it away. Perel, seeing her hard work being stolen, cried out in distress and ran to block the soldier's way. With pleading eyes she beseeched him to return the bread.

Astonished at her temerity, the soldier softened. He searched in his pockets for a coin to toss at her. Failing to find one, he declared that he would return in a day or two to pay for the bread. To appease her, he pulled something out of his bag to serve as collateral.

"Here," he called, pulling out a small pillow. "This is booty — booty from the enemy. If I don't return within three days, sell it and live off the proceeds!" The last words floated away on the wind as the soldier galloped off on his horse in a cloud of dust.

When Perel picked up the pillow, it felt strangely heavy to her. Inspecting it, she saw a great many stitches in the pillow's fabric. Upon her return home later, she related the incident to her parents. Her father, hefting the pillow, suggested that she open it, but Perel was adamant about waiting the three days. The pillow, she said, had been given to her as collateral. It would not be hers until three days passed with no sign of the soldier.

Three days passed, but the soldier never returned. With her parents looking on curiously, Perel took a knife and began slitting the pillow's seams. Suddenly — like something out of a dream — large gold coins began pouring out of the pillow.

The hovel was shaken by inarticulate cries. Gold coins rolled about on the wooden floor as three pairs of eyes looked on in disbelief. Slowly, the tears came, and finally joy stepped in to replace the bewilderment.

Reb Shmelka was the first to regain his wits. In a ringing voice he pronounced a prayer of thanksgiving to Hashem. Then he called for paper and ink. There was another letter to be written to his future son-in-law, announcing the wonderful news — that Hashem had heard their prayers and restored his wealth.

The way was clear for Perel's marriage to R' Leib — the extraordinary young man who later came to be known as the Maharal of Prague.

❧ The Prognosis

R' Shraga Feivel Frank was a kind and wealthy man. Part of his property took the form of apartments for rent. Out of the goodness of his heart, R' Feivel often filled these apartments with hapless folk who were unable to pay. To relieve them of any distress, he devised a strategy that took him around to each of these apartments, secretly, on a monthly basis. Each *Rosh Chodesh* eve he would hide a sum equal to the rent money under the tablecloths of these tenants. When he came around again to collect the rent, they would pay him with this money, never dreaming that his had been the hand that had placed it there.

R' Feivel's reputation spread far and wide. When his daughters reached marriageable age, it was no surprise to anyone when he insisted that they marry only genuine Torah scholars. His wishes in this matter, sadly, were to be fulfilled in posthumous form; he died when he was only 45. Before he died, he explained to his wife that the full responsibility for finding appropriate husbands for their daughters was hers.

The first son-in-law was the *gaon* R' Moshe Mordechai Epstein, *Rosh Yeshivah* of Hevron. For the second daughter, Baila Hinda, her uncle sought the cream of the yeshivah crop. Traveling to Volozhin, he let it be known that he wanted the best boy in the yeshivah.

There was no doubt in any mind about the identity of that particular young man: R' Isser Zalman Meltzer. After some preliminary talk, R' Isser Zalman brought the suggestion to his two *rebbeim*, R' Chaim Soloveitchik and the Netziv. Both gave their blessing to the match, and the *shidduch* was finalized.

R' Isser Zalman's terrible financial situation was well known, though he tried not to let his poverty show. For his engagement, he borrowed a coat from one of his fellow yeshivah students. This *shidduch* would propel him into a household that would care for his every physical need. The maxim that Torah would emerge from the ranks of the poor proved itself in his case.

For a period after the engagement, he learned in Radin. The yeshivah rented a room for him in the house of a dairy worker, who sorely needed the money that a tenant would bring in. The man's difficulty in earning a livelihood led him to a decision to deal in ox hides. Before he could sell them, the hides had to be dried and tanned, and he elected to do the drying on the windowsills of his home — including the one in R' Isser Zalman's room. Once the hides had dried, he would store them all in R' Isser Zalman's room, where they gave off a noxious and unhealthy odor. R' Isser Zalman was reluctant to inform the yeshivah authorities about this, lest they refuse to continue renting the room and the dairyman's livelihood suffer. He therefore kept silent.

It was at this point in his life that R' Isser Zalman contracted tuberculosis. The illness sent him home, where he grew progressively weaker. Just when there seemed no solution in sight, Hashem, in His kindness, sent one. An outbreak of fire resulted in a number of injured and ill who had to be evacuated from the town — and R' Isser Zalman with them. Caring people rented a room for him on a farm, where he enjoyed fresh milk and complete rest. The healthy forest air worked its own magic upon the convalescent. Slowly he began to grow a little stronger, though his condition was still far from good.

His high standard of integrity prompted R' Isser Zalman to send a letter to the Franks, his *kallah's* family, informing them of his illness and offering them the option of rescinding the *shidduch.* He soon received a letter by return mail, urging him to come to them in Kovno, a city that boasted many doctors. The Franks paid for his medical care and then, on the doctors' advice, sent him to a forest spa to recuperate.

Fearful people began whispering in the bride's ear: "It would be better to be free of this match. What do you need with a sickly husband?" But Baila Hinda knew that to abandon this *shidduch* would be to incur an eternal loss, and she refused to listen to the advice of the anxious.

When the pressure on her increased and the whisperings became open, she personally visited the doctors to ask about her *chasan's* prognosis. Was there any chance of his living a normal life span in his condition? They returned a sorrowful shake of the head. R' Isser Zalman, the doctors told the girl, could live one year at the most.

With fortitude and conviction, she drew herself up and declared, "To live with such a *talmid chacham* for one year is a special privilege. I will not give up the *shidduch!*" She was determined to care for him devotedly and clung to the hope that, with Hashem's help, R' Isser Zalman's life would be long and healthy.

Her family continued urging her to change her mind. She could have her pick of fine young men — men of excellent character and healthy bodies — men of sterling quality! Finally, Baila Hinda decided to ask the Chofetz Chaim for his opinion. She went to see him and poured out the story. After listening attentively, the Chofetz Chaim murmured, "There are people who are healthy, and there are people who live long."

These words were enough to send Baila Hinda home with renewed determination to resist her family's importunities. In due time she married her betrothed — and lived with him for 60 years. R' Isser Zalman's soul did not return to its Maker until he had reached the ripe old age of 84!

✊ The Long Engagement

R' Chaim Chaikin grew up in the shadow of the Chofetz Chaim. After years of learning in Radin, he moved to Baranovich to study under R' Elchonon Wasserman. Then the yeshivah at Strassburg, France, decided that he incorporated the precise qualities they were seeking in a *Rosh Yeshivah*. The previous *Rosh Yeshivah* had left, and they were actively searching for a replacement. With R' Chaim's love of Torah and love for his fellow Jew, he was the best man for the job.

He was received at the yeshivah with open arms. His students soon came to adore him. In a short time, R' Chaim and the yeshivah became a single sterling edifice.

As a French citizen, R' Chaim was drafted into the army for a period of several months. He arrived in the city of Nancy, one Jewish soldier among a great many Gentile ones. Without kosher food on his base, R' Chaim was forced to seek sustenance at a Jewish home nearby. He turned to the Slovotzkys, a pious and warm-hearted family that took him in. R' Chaim also spent his free time lecturing to the local Jews, the model and epitome of a genuine *ben Torah*.

When a match was suggested between R' Chaim and Fraidel Slovotzky, the daughter of the house, he responded with a willing "Yes," knowing that Fraidel aspired to be a true helpmate for a husband totally immersed in the life of Torah. The engagement took place in Nancy, to the accompaniment of widespread joy.

But Heaven had decreed that the wedding itself would be delayed. World War II broke out at that juncture and R' Chaim

Chaikin was sent to the battlefront, where he was captured by the Germans. This proved to be his salvation, for by spending all the war years inside prison walls he escaped the long hand of the Nazi death machine.

His bride sent him letters in prison — letters filled with love of Torah and *yiras Shamayim*. He was willing to free her of the obligation to marry him, but she remained firm in her commitment. He was the man, she said, with whom she had chosen to climb the ladder of Torah and Divine aspiration. She was prepared to wait for him as long as necessary. Her exile to Montevideo, Uruguay, together with her family, did not stop the steady exchange of letters to and from prison, or put an end to the food packages Fraidel faithfully sent her *chasan* to sweeten his imprisonment.

Local Uruguayan Jews were persistent in urging her to marry various successful young men in the community. Why wait so long for someone who might never return? But Fraidel had no interest in successful young men, only in a Torah scholar whose success was measured by an eternal standard. With R' Chaim, she would realize her spiritual ambitions. The war wore on. She continued to wait.

After five long years, R' Chaim was released at last from his German prison. He made his way directly to the yeshivah in France that had become so central to his being, and quickly wrote a letter to his bride, asking her to join him there. Visas were hard to come by in Uruguay in those days, and ships were few. Fraidel might have insisted that he come to Uruguay and take up a rabbinical position there, but she came to understand that he wished to devote his life to the yeshivah he loved and to teaching Torah to French Jews thirsty for knowledge of their heritage.

It was a full year before she was able to find a place on a ship bound for France — but when that ship left port, Fraidel was aboard.

Seven years had elapsed between the engagement and the wedding. For seven years, Fraidel had kept her vision firmly fixed on her betrothed's fine qualities and eminent spiritual accomplishments. For seven years, she had demonstrated her willingness to sacrifice everything for the sake of living in a place of Torah, and for the sake of seeing her husband rise ever higher in his service of Hashem, as he taught his numerous students in Yeshivah Aix-les-Bains.

After the wedding, the couple was allotted a single room, where they lived under extremely cramped and uncomfortable conditions. They had no kitchen and no bathroom. The barest essentials for physical existence were missing, but — and this was more important — the essentials for a thriving spiritual life were present in abundance. Fraidel accepted every difficulty with complete contentment.

Their entire life was bound up in the yeshivah. Rebbetzin Chaikin became the "yeshivah mother" in the fullest sense of the word. She worried about each student and cared for his individual needs. By her order, ailing boys received special meals. Those whose homes were located at a great distance from the yeshivah found a substitute mother in the Rebbetzin during yeshivah vacations.

The jewel in Rebbetzin Fraidel's crown was her absolute devotion to Torah. While still engaged, she had written her *chasan* a letter in which she expressed the hope that she might not be the cause of more than the barest minimum of time lost from his Torah study. At the start of their life together, R' Chaim had requested that he not be bound by mealtimes, so that he might always be available for the yeshivah. Sometimes a student needed to be spoken to, or a member of the staff; a man as dedicated as R' Chaim was bound to find himself delayed at frequent intervals. The Rebbetzin, of course, consented to this request, and often waited hours until her husband appeared at home. Then, without a word of reproach, she would heat his meal and serve it to him with a smile. This was her mission. Her husband had his important work to do, and she had hers.

In this special atmosphere, R' Chaim Chaikin was able to realize his full potential and become one of the Torah giants of his generation. He left his indelible stamp on French Jewry and raised numerous students who went on to spread Torah, in France and in the world at large.

≈ A Dream Come True

Rebbetzin Bousilla, wife of the *gaon* R' Ezra Attia, possessed a love of Torah that was legendary. In her youth, before she met her future husband but after his name had already been suggested to her as a possible match, she had a dream in which she saw a Torah scroll approaching her. In the morning, when she awoke, she realized that Heaven had handed her a hint: Ezra Attia, the Torah scholar, was the husband for her. Indeed, a *sefer Torah* had moved her way.

The engagement took place on *Rosh Chodesh* Adar 5668 (1908). Her father, the *mekubal* R' Avraham Selim, signed the *tena'im* on behalf of his daughter. R' Ezra Attia, an orphan, signed on his own behalf.

On the 11th day of Nissan, the eve of *Shabbos HaGadol,* the couple were married in Jerusalem and took up residence in a one-room apartment in Jerusalem's Bucharim section. Lacking almost everything in the way of material goods, they set out to build a Torah home.

Bousilla acquired an ancient sewing machine and earned their meager living by sewing and mending clothes so that her husband might spend all his time immersed in Torah. Her mother-in-law lived with them during this time, taking upon herself some of the housework to help lighten the burden on her daughter-in-law. In that home, R' Ezra grew to tremendous stature, and was selected to head the Porat Yosef Yeshivah in Jerusalem.

A wife completely devoted to Torah — and the home that that wife created — had made all the difference.

Part Twelve:
A Mother's Inspiration

✺ Her Son's Champion

BEHIND MANY TORAH GIANTS STANDS A DEVOUT Jewish mother — a woman whose fervent dream is to see her son light up the sky of the Jewish nation with Torah. Her prayers cascade from the heart like water down a mountain, as she beseeches her Creator to help her sons grow in Torah and piety. She pinches pennies and goes without so that the finest tutors might be hired to teach her children.

Such a woman was Chaya Wachs, mother of R' Chaim Eliezer Wachs. Immediately upon his birth, she began praying for his success in learning Torah. She carried the infant from one *gadol* to another, collecting blessings for the child. And, to her joy, these Torah greats assured her that the boy was destined for greatness.

Chaya was totally committed to her son's success. Not content to rely on blessings and prayers, she did everything she could to ease his way in learning. No sacrifice was too great to consider. Once, when the boy was only 4, he fell gravely ill and the doctors despaired of his life. Chaya prayed up to Hashem, telling Him that she was prepared to give half the years of her own life in order to save her son's.

Her prayers were heard. Within hours, the boy began to recover — and, at the same time, his mother fell ill. For long months she hovered between life and death, until Hashem, in His great kindness, restored her to health.

As the boy matured, Chaya urged her son to enter the rabbinate. R' Chaim Eliezer relates how his mother stood by his side at every turn of the road, helping him along. She championed his causes and fought a vociferous member of his congregation who continually embittered the young rabbi's life. The fight destroyed Chaya's health and led to her demise.

After his mother's passing, R' Chaim Eliezer decided to dedicate his learning to the woman who had done more than anybody to facilitate his rise in Torah. And when he published his famous work, it was entitled *"Nefesh Chayah."*

✿ The Fruits of Her Labor

A burning love for Torah was ever in the heart of R' Chaim of Volozhin's mother. A number of stories have been told about this remarkable woman.

It is said that after she provided the town Rabbi — the Sha'agas Aryeh — with a fine set of the Talmud, he blessed her, saying that she would give birth to two additional sons. One of these, he predicted, would disseminate *Shas* throughout the world, while the other would not require a *Shas* — he would have it all committed to memory. The first son was R' Chaim, founder of the Volozhin Yeshivah, and the second was R' Zalman, who never forgot a word he learned.

As it happened, the Sha'agas Aryeh was staying at her house when her pains presaging the birth of R' Chaim began. In order not to disturb the Rabbi's study, she suffered the pains in silence. When informed that a son had been born, the Sha'agas Aryeh blessed the child, saying that he would rise to greatness until the voice of his Torah was heard in the streets. There are those who add that it was not a coincidence that the Rabbi was at the house at that particular time; the mother had asked him to come so that the very first sounds her baby would hear in this world would be sounds of Torah.

R' Chaim himself tells of his mother's extreme modesty. All her life she toiled and struggled to instruct her sons in Torah and mitzvos, dreaming of greatness for them. In *Toldas Adam*, his book about his brother, the holy R' Zalman, R' Chaim writes of the way his exemplary parents did everything in their power to make the Torah beloved to their sons and directed them always to strive for perfection. They hired outstanding teachers for their boys and took them to the local rabbis so that they might hear words of Torah from their lips. When their oldest son, R' Simcha, completed all six tractates of the *Mishnah* and knew them by heart, his parents held a festive party to help him appreciate his learning even more. His younger brother, Zalman, saw all the excitement and was jealous. He vowed that he would do the same thing as his big brother — and he would begin at once. He was only 4 years old at the time!

They had five sons, every one of them a superlative Torah scholar. Apart from the two more famous sons, R' Chaim and R' Zalman, the other three — R' Simcha, R' Nachman and R' Yosef — served as rabbis and teachers in prominent communities throughout Lithuania and Poland.

🦋 Only the Best

R' Meir Dan Plotzki was born in Kutna in the year 5626 (1866) to R' Chaim Yitzchak and his wife Gella. As he grew, his unusual talents were revealed. From the very start, his parents strove to plant a deep love of Torah in his heart.

At the age of 3, Meir fell ill. He grew steadily weaker, until the doctors despaired of his life. His father, R' Chaim Yitzchak, traveled to the Alexander Rebbe to plead for a blessing. "He will have a *refuah sheleimah*," the Rebbe said. Then he added, "You will reap much *nachas* from him, because he will grow to be a great rabbi."

The father returned to Kutna clutching tightly to the memory of this blessing, secure in the belief that his son would recover from his illness. And, indeed, the boy's health improved until he was fully recovered.

As soon as Meir was well, his parents dedicated him to Torah. They hired the best tutors, men who could actualize the splendid potential they saw in the boy. But the financial drain was extremely difficult. R' Chaim Yitzchak dealt with lumber merchants, a business that brought in only a meager income and also forced them to move from time to time, to be near the forests.

Husband and wife were consumed with anxiety about their son's future. No tutor worth his wages would agree to keep moving from one forest to another — and when it came to their Meir's learning, they would have only the best. Finally, they decided for their son's sake to invest everything they owned in acquiring a fine teacher who would agree to accompany them in their travels. The boy should not have to miss even one day of learning.

They found just the right person, and paid him lavishly. When the last of their money was gone, Gella sold her jewelry. She paid part of the proceeds to the current teacher and kept some in reserve for future teachers. Their son, Meir, grew in Torah, and in the course of time became a rabbi and *Rosh Yeshivah*. He became famous through his work, *Klei Chemdah*, a commentary on the Torah. And when his mother left this world, he eulogized her with these ringing words: "My Torah is your Torah!"

❧ The Birth of the Rebbe of Ostrow

In the small town of Sabin, near Poland's capital city of Warsaw, a son was born to the *chassid* R' Avraham Yitzchak HaLevi Halstock and his wife, Chana Baila. Eight days after he was born, he entered into the covenant of Israel and was named Meir Yechiel.

While Chana Baila was expecting, she suddenly fell ill and sensed that something was wrong with her child. The doctors feared that the matter posed a life-threatening risk to the mother, and felt that it was impossible for both the mother and baby to survive.

She went to R' Yehoshua of Zelechov, son of the "Holy Yid" of P'shische, to ask his opinion. He suggested that she go to shul during the reading of the Torah portion and *daven*. She made her way to the shul, where she stood and prayed silently. At the very moment the ark was opened and the *sefer Torah* taken out, she suddenly felt better.

Chana Baila hurried back to the Rebbe and told him what had occurred. The Rebbe assured her: "You are carrying not only a son, but a jewel that will one day light up the world."

R' Avraham Yitzchak was very poor and worked strenuously for his living. He traveled regularly to R' Yehoshua's brother, R' Yerachmiel, and also to R' Meir Yechiel of Muglenzia, seeking their advice on all matters spiritual and material. His good wife, Chana Baila, did likewise.

A pretzel baker, R' Avraham Yitzchak could afford no better housing than a wooden shack consisting of a single room. In this room he ate, slept, learned and baked his bagel-like pretzels. Every night, while the rest of Sabin was plunged into deep sleep, he and his wife rose at 2 a.m. to begin kneading and shaping their dough. The oven was lit and the trays of pretzels inserted. When the baking was done, R' Avraham Yitzchak filled two large baskets with pretzels and left the house before dawn, the heavy baskets on his back, to make his way to the neighboring villages to sell his wares.

In a corner of that simple room, close by the warm oven, was young Meir Yechiel. Even when very small, he would awaken when his parents did, and watch the way his parents worked to knead and shape and bake their pretzels. While they baked, R' Avraham Yitzchak circled the room and recited *Tehillim*. The people of Sabin used to say that R' Avraham Yitzchak kneaded his pretzels with psalms.

Little Meir Yechiel sat in his corner and watched, eyes hooded with sleepiness. When his father's pacing took him close to the boy, R' Avraham Yitzchak would reach down to cup the boy's two smooth cheeks with his hands and say, "Remember this, my son. The better sealed an oven is, the more heat it will have."

From time to time the little boy would try to help with the work, willing his small hands to knead and shape the pretzels. And as he worked, he would repeat the lesson his father had taught him: "The better sealed an oven is, the more heat it will have."

Later, Meir Yechiel began accompanying his father on the rounds of the villages. On their return, father and son entered the *beis midrash* and spent several hours learning before the morning prayers. In the women's section stood Chana Baila, drenching her *Korban Minchah siddur* with her tears, pouring out her dreams and hopes for her son.

Her prayers were answered. Meir Yechiel grew up to become the rebbe of Ostrow, revered far and wide as the "*Gaon* of Ostrow."

🐾 Mother of a Dynasty

Rivka Miriam, wife of the first Belzer Rebbe, spent a great deal of her time performing acts of kindness and distributing charitable monies. One *erev Shabbos*, her husband, R' Yehoshua, heard Rivka Miriam weeping in her room. When he sent someone in to ask what was wrong, she said that she did not have sufficient funds that week to distribute to the poor as was her custom. All week long she had clung to the hope that the money would be found, yet here it was, just before candle-lighting on Friday, and she had still not obtained the money. She sobbed as if her heart would break.

Hearing this, R' Yehoshua sent back word that if she was prepared to give him some sort of collateral, he would lend her the amount missing from her usual weekly sum. The Rebbetzin brightened, and immediately sent him her ornate head ker-chief as collateral. Money in hand, she hurried jubilantly to deliver it to several needy families before Shabbos. Then she returned home to light her own candles in joy and content-ment.

Watching her, R' Yehoshua pointed at their son, Yissachar Dov, and remarked, "If one lights candles in such a manner, it is no wonder that one merits such sons!"

Rivka Miriam became the mother of the Belzer dynasty, personally raising her son to be the next Belzer Rebbe.

❧ And You Have Surpassed Them All

There are few who have not heard of R' Meir Shapiro, *Rosh Yeshivah* of Yeshivah Chochmei Lublin and innovator of the *daf yomi* concept. His brilliance and stature are a byword. R' Meir often spoke of his mother's role in his young life. His father, R' Yaakov Shimshon, apparently recognized his wife's superlative qualities as well. He would recite the line, "Many daughters have amassed achievement, but you have surpassed them all," and then add, "She whose love for Torah burns inside has produced fruits worthy of her."

R' Meir, whose talents were evident even from a young age, was particularly impressed by an incident that occurred when he was just seven years old. One day after *isru chag* Pesach 5654 (1894), he found his mother in tears. Anxiously, he asked her why she was crying.

"Before Pesach, we hired a teacher — an outstanding *talmid chacham* from Sochachov — for you, and agreed to pay him the generous sum of 300 rubles, in addition to his room and board, for the *zeman*. And now," she said with a doleful sigh, "here it is, two days after the holiday, and he hasn't appeared." The tears welled up in her eyes as she added earnestly, "My son, every day that passes without learning Torah is an irretrievable loss. Who knows — Maybe the salary we offered was too low. It's a sacrifice for us, no negligible amount, but for the sake of the precious Torah it is only a small sacrifice."

Her spirits lifted when the teacher knocked at their door that very day. R' Shalom of Sochachov taught Meir for the next six years.

But his mother was not destined to see her son at the height of his glory. During the dark days of World War I, on the 24th day of Nissan 5675 (1915), her soul returned to its Maker. But R' Meir never forgot her kindness to him in his youth.

His student, R' Yitzchak Flakser, related: "Once, when addressing a huge crowd in Poland, R' Meir surprised his audience by crying out, very emotionally, 'Rejoice, my mother, in *Gan Eden*. Be happy. See what greatness and honor your son has merited, growing up to become a leader in Israel!' The audience was bewildered and taken aback by this manner of describing himself. Then R' Meir turned to the women's section and cried: 'And you, women of Israel, proper Jewish mothers — if you also wish your sons to grow up to be *gaonim* and rabbis, walk in the footsteps of my mother, who sacrificed to raise her son for the Torah.'"

❧ A Deserving Woman

R' Aryeh Ze'ev HaCohen, father of the Chofetz Chaim, was a storekeeper who always put Torah first. He married the modest and humble Dobrusha. The Chofetz Chaim's biography relates that his mother was extremely careful in all her mitzvah observances, both large and small. In honor of the Shabbos she would light many candles and scrupulously observe every stricture. She did not carry so much as a house key outside her home, even when there was an *eruv*. Her entire Shabbos was one of spiritual elevation, with hours spent poring over her *Chumash* and *Tehillim* and *midrashim*.

Dobrusha was a private person who spent much of her time in solitude. She spoke about no one, and stayed far from groups where idle chatter was commonplace. "I sat alone," she would quote, "and my soul was whole."

She personally taught her son to read from the *siddur*. On

one occasion, when asked how she had merited such a child, she replied in all humility, "I am just a Jewish woman like all other Jewish women, but if Hashem has granted him to me, I suppose I deserved to have him."

The Chofetz Chaim's sister's *chasan* found an old volume of *Tehillim* in his in-laws' home. It had belonged to Dobrusha, the Chofetz Chaim's mother. The young man brought it to the Chofetz Chaim, who wept as he kissed it, and said, "You will never know how many tears my mother, may her memory be blessed, shed over this *Tehillim*. Every day, before dawn, she would pour out her heart to Hashem, pleading for her son to grow into a good and upright Jew."

It should come as no surprise to anyone that such a mother produced such a son!

❧ True Nachas

Rabbi Elya Lopian relates the following:

"During World War I, we reached the point where we were hungry for bread. Neighbors of ours who had sons in yeshivos sent word for their boys to come home and find some sort of work so that they could earn money for food to stave off starvation. We had nine sons, all learning in yeshivah, but their mother would not hear of their leaving yeshivah, even for an hour.

"The neighbors asked her, 'Why are you suffering so much? Summon one, two, or three of your sons home and let them chase away hunger for the rest of you!'

"Forcefully, the Rebbetzin answered, 'I don't want my sons' help now. There will come a time when I will really need their help — and that's in the World to Come. That's why I want them to remain in yeshivah now — so that they'll be able to help me when I need it!'"

Rabbi Lopian concludes: "When my wife passed away in England, I was the 10th in the *minyan* as our sons went to her grave to learn *mishnayos* and say *Kaddish*. She must indeed enjoy a great deal of *nachas* from her sons."

❧ The Road Not Taken

R' Yosef Chaim Sonnenfeld lost his father, R' Avraham Shlomo, at the tender age of 6. This tragedy, and its consequences, left their indelible mark on the boy's life.

His mother, the righteous Zelda, accepted the decree and stoically undertook to be both mother and father to her three children. To support them, she peddled merchandise through the town, always bearing her suffering with dignity. So strong was her faith in Hashem that the moment Zelda had earned enough for the week's food, she would fold up her cart and stay home to be with her children.

For two years she carried the heavy load alone, trying with all her might to swallow her pain and reconcile herself to her fate. Finally, physically weakened and broken in spirit, Zelda realized that she needed help in ensuring the proper upbringing for her children. When a respected man was suggested as a match for her, a man prepared to care for her children, she agreed to marry him.

After the wedding, the family moved to Semenitz, where her new husband maintained his residence. Her son was placed in the local Talmud Torah, but by law he was required to attend the secular school as well. There, his extraordinary abilities brought him to the attention of his teachers. He was particularly brilliant in mathematics; hardly had the teacher posed a question than young Chaim was ready with the solution. Once, the teacher presented a particularly difficult problem and gave the class three hours to come up with the answer. As soon as he finished speaking, a smile spread over Chaim's face and his eyes twinkled mischievously. The teacher, noticing this, thought he had his chance to exact payment for all the times the boy had confounded him by dismissing his questions with a wave of a hand.

"*Nu*, Chaim," he demanded, "will you solve this problem so easily?"

Blushing modestly, Chaim said, "How is this problem different from the others? I don't see any special difficulty here." As he spoke, he presented the solution to the problem in its entirety — to the teacher's utter stupefaction!

But his secular studies were secondary to his Torah learning. Here, too, he became famous for his abilities. His diligence was extraordinary for a boy of his age. He found no lure in childish games, devoting every free minute to reading. It is said that 8 year-old Chaim used the time between their arrival in Semenitz and his enrollment in the local school to fill the margins of *Sha'arei Zion on Tefillah* with comments and numerical calculations (*gematrios*). He then wrote a poem, in rhyme, on the topic of prayer.

At the age of 11, he graduated from school with honors, and concluded his studies in the Talmud Torah as well. His secular-studies teachers managed to convince his well-meaning stepfather that a boy of Chaim's abilities should continue his higher education. If he did, they prophesied, Chaim would astound the world with his brilliance one day, perhaps becoming a renowned scientist. Chaim's older brother, caught up in the spirit of the times, agreed with this assessment. Both his brother and his stepfather were of one mind: to transfer Chaim to a secular high school.

Knowing Chaim's purity and idealism, they tried to conceal their plans from him. When the time came, they would present him with a *fait accompli*. But he soon learned of it, and set about trying to devise his own plan for foiling theirs at any price.

For days the boy went around depressed and anxious, searching for a way out of his troubles. He knew that he did not stand much chance of bending his stepfather's will, especially if it was supported by his own brother. In those difficult times, when yeshivah students were forced to care for their own needs and find their meals at the townspeople's tables, it would be all but impossible for an orphan such as Chaim — without some person of means prepared to support him — to obtain a place in one of the various yeshivos that were sprinkled throughout Hungary and Slovakia.

Zelda, aware of the plans being set into motion for her beloved son, wept secretly at the thought of his being removed from a place of Torah. She knew her son well, and anticipated greatness from him. With bitter tears she beseeched her Creator to raise her Chaim'l to Torah and fear of Heaven. Seeing the boy's anguished face, she urged him to confide in her. He spilled out his despair at the plans his stepfather and brother were making for his future — then discovered with delight that his mother agreed completely with his own view of the matter. He had merely begun to taste the Torah's sweetness; it was now his sole ambition to continue growing in Torah.

The mother was awed at the young boy's profound under-standing of life's true values. Shedding tears of joy, she hugged her son and promised to do everything in her power to see that he continued his yeshivah studies. She confided that all her hopes for him had always been, and would always be, centered on his growth in Torah. This, she said, would comfort her for all that she had endured since the death of her first husband, Chaim's father.

An idea sprouted, crystallized and then took root. She would send Chaim to a small yeshivah located in his home town of Verbau. Her son would *not* attend a secular high school — not if she had her way!

At that time, the *tzaddik* R' Yehudah Asad was passing through Semenitz. In communities throughout Hungary and Slovakia, Jews flocked to meet this holy man, their leader for the past 20 years. Through his yeshivah for outstanding stu-dents, R' Asad had transformed the area into a thriving hub of

Torah. His coming aroused an excitement that quickly reached fever pitch.

When the *tzaddik* arrived at his inn, an eager throng of men, women and children were on hand to welcome him. Fathers lifted their children onto their shoulders to receive his blessing, which had been proven to have amazing powers. A child blessed by R' Asad would never depart from the Torah.

Fatigued from his journey, the *tzaddik* had to refrain from receiving petitioners. The crowd persisted for a time, still aflame with hope. Among them was a young boy. He did not have shoulders to sit on, for his father had been gathered to his ancestors years before, in Verbau. The boy was buffeted by the masses of people and nearly trampled time and again, but he persisted in his desire for a glimpse of the *tzaddik's* face.

At last, the disappointed crowd began to thin, until only the orphaned boy remained. With all the strength of his young obstinacy, he refused to leave without the *tzaddik's* blessing. Somehow, R' Asad heard about him. To the astonishment of his entourage, he called for the boy. Teeth chattering with fear and awe, Chaim approached the *tzaddik*. One trembling hand reached out to touch the great man's. R' Asad embraced the boy warmly and asked his name. Upon hearing that he was a grandson of the *gaon*, R' Shmuel Nadish, he spread his hands over the boy's head and blessed him with great affection.

From that time on, it was as though new life had been breathed into Chaim. Armed with that blessing, he no longer had doubts about choosing the yeshivah life. For the rest of his life he would recall the special moment when the *tzaddik* rested his hands on his young head and bestowed his blessing.

From his graduation from elementary school at the age of 11 until he became bar mitzvah, Chaim continued his learning with the Semenitz Rav, R' Yehudah Leib Lefler. In the meantime, he prepared in earnest for the realization of his dream, to enter a yeshivah — a project in which his mother was secretly lending a hand. She had adjured him to wait until his bar mitzvah, and that date took on an added significance in his mind. It would mark the start of a new era, a time when he would be a man responsible for himself and under no obligation to bow to the wishes of anyone who might want to choose his future path. Not surprisingly, his whole being was focused on his bar mitzvah with a sense of overwhelming anticipation. No months or weeks had ever seemed longer. He had merited, Chaim would joke, the privilege of "long years of life" while still in his childhood.

At last, the great day arrived: *Rosh Chodesh* Cheshvan, 5622 (1861). Both Chaim and his mother passed a sleepless and emotional night. When daylight arrived, Chaim jumped out of bed and tiptoed over to his mother's room to see if she was awake. Before he got there, he discerned faint sounds from the kitchen. He found his mother bent over her *siddur* by the light of a small kerosene lamp, pouring out her heart in a whisper as her tears fell onto the venerable yellowed pages.

The bar mitzvah boy stood watching her from the doorway, almost beside himself with the profound emotion that the sight aroused in him. It was as though all the years that the orphan and widow had experienced together were telescoped into that one moment. Then, suddenly, his mother became aware of his presence. Her warm, maternal gaze fell on her son. Now that the time had come to part with her precious jewel, her heart wrenched with pain. She found herself beset by doubts and worries. Would a lone orphan boy be capable of withstanding all the ordeals he would face in yeshivah? Picturing all the difficulties he would meet, she wished to prepare him. At the same time, more than anything, the mother wanted to sweep her chick under her wing and keep him safe. Groping for the right words, she spoke to him about what lay ahead.

When she had finished, a deep silence reigned in the kitchen, as the mother witnessed her son's silent turmoil. Suddenly, she found a new strength.

"Well, my darling?" she asked. "What have you decided? Where are you going?"

"To Verbau!" Chaim answered quietly, but with a determination that acknowledged no obstacle.

After *davening* with the sunrise and snatching a quick breakfast, Chaim picked up his knapsack, slung it over his shoulders, and — together with his mother and a friend his own age — left Semenitz. As they walked, the mother murmured psalms for her son's safety on the long road to Verbau.

When they had left the city limits, Chaim pleaded with his mother to turn back. With kind, loving and sensible words he soothed her troubled spirit. It was as though he had grown overnight into a wise and mature young man. He concluded with confidence that Hashem, Guardian of orphans, would lead him safely to his destination. His mother stopped, planted a trembling kiss on his forehead and parted from her son with tear-filled eyes.

For Chaim, that was the beginning of the road to greatness. He grew in Torah and succeeded in attaining the stature of a *gaon* and leader in his generation — R' Yosef Chaim Sonnenfeld, Rabbi of Jerusalem.

✖ Companion to Torah

The Grossbard family of Vesin, Lithuania, found itself suddenly and tragically bereft of its father. R' Aharon Ze'ev Grossbard, though young in years, had been one of the giants of the *beis midrash* in Kelm. But his star had no sooner begun to rise than his sun set before its time. He was asked to testify to the authorities against a Jew — and refused. Consequently, he was beaten to death, leaving his wife a widow and his children, orphans.

The bereft mother dedicated every ounce of strength left her to the job of upholding and supporting her three children. The oldest was Shraga Tzvi, who subsequently became renowned in

Lithuanian yeshivos and bore a good name throughout his lifetime as he served as general director of the Chinuch Atzma'i movement. His two brothers, Abba and Shmuel, were enveloped in Shraga Tzvi's love of Torah. And it was their mother who strove, morning, noon and night, to inculcate all three sons with love of Torah, love of Hashem and fear of Heaven.

It was no easy task to master her own anguish and act as both mother and father to her sons. With steadfast faith and staunch persistence, she succeeded at that daunting job. She raised her boys to be fine Jews — Jews whose dedication to Torah remained with them all their lives. And the journey began with the daily trip to *cheder*.

This was a *cheder* in the old-fashioned sense of the word. A single teacher instructed boys of various ages. Every hour, a different group learned with the teacher while the rest studied on their own. Classes were held in a different home each day. Friday, *erev Shabbos,* was a day that most families found it difficult to host the *cheder* boys; that was when the class learned at the Grossbard home. Mrs. Grossbard welcomed them with radiant affection, watching benevolently as the young boys learned until 1 o'clock.

On other days, the *cheder* began after *Shacharis* and ended when the kerosene in the lamp ran out. Sometimes this was earlier, sometimes later. As long as the light lasted, the children of Wizhan, including three Grossbard boys, learned.

When Mrs. Grossbard saw that the time had come for her sons to move on to larger Torah centers, she sent them to a yeshivah near Bialystok. In order to be closer to them, she gave up her small fabric business and moved to the town as well. She did the same thing when her sons went to learn in Grodno, always accompanying them on their road to Torah heights. And always, she made certain to live close to the *beis midrash*, so that the sound of Torah rang perpetually in her children's ears.

In the latter part of her life, Mrs. Grossbard moved to *Eretz Yisrael,* where she continued to live near her sons and to glimpse her reward during her lifetime. She passed away in the year 5723 (1963). Her funeral procession passed near the Ponovizh Yeshivah, where the *mashgiach*, R' Yechezkel Levinstein, eulogized her. "I have good news for you — your portion in the World to Come is ready and prepared."

Whoever knew how carefully the *mashgiach* always weighed his words went away deeply impressed with that righteous woman's deeds.

☙ A Mother's Tears

The Chazon Ish once answered a student's question with the following:

"You should know that there are many ways of finding merit. A boy without remarkable abilities may nevertheless try hard and achieve success — all in the merit of a mother or grandmother or even a great-grandmother who, as she lit the Shabbos candles, let fall a warm tear or two as she prayed from the depths of her heart that her descendants might be Torah scholars and rise to heights in Torah. The merit of that mother or grandmother's tears assists that boy to become great in Torah."

❧ A Prayer Answered

On the 11th of Cheshvan, the day of Rachel *Imeinu's* *yahrtzeit*, R' Chaim Shmulevitz went to pray at her tomb. From the other side, he heard a woman praying for children. "Mother Rachel, you yourself knew the bitterness of being childless. Please, Mother, speak up on my behalf — that I might have living children."

R' Chaim became very emotional upon hearing this prayer. "I am sure that these words will be accepted on high. Next year, I would like to be the *sandak* at that *bris*." He proceeded to find out the woman's identity. And, sure enough, the following year, R' Chaim served as *sandak* at the *bris* of that woman's newborn son.

❧ No Sacrifice Too Great

The Ridbaz, R' Yaakov Dovid Willowski, spent the last years of his life in the holy city of Tzefas. Prior to that, he had served as the rabbi of Slutsk, Poland, and composed a commentary on parts of the Talmud Yerushalmi. He was considered one of the great scholars of his generation.

It was a cold winter's day in Tzefas, and it was his father's *yahrtzeit*. That afternoon, the Ridbaz arrived at shul for *Minchah* earlier than usual, before most of the others had arrived. He walked over to a *shtender* and rested his elbows on it, lost in thought. Tears quickly formed in his eyes and he began to weep in earnest.

The shul gradually filled. Knowing that the Ridbaz had *yahrtzeit*, the other men kept their distance. But one close friend came over and said, "Why is the Rav so sad? The Rav's father was 80 years old when he passed away — certainly not a young man — and his passing took place nearly 50 years ago."

The Ridbaz looked at him and said quietly, "I will tell you." He began his story.

"I was thinking about the time when I was a young boy and my father arranged for the best teacher in town, R' Chaim Sender, to be my private tutor. His fee was one ruble per month — a huge sum in those days, especially for my father, who was a poor man. Coming up with that amount of money every month was a real challenge for him.

"My father earned his living building ovens. One winter, there was a shortage of mortar and lime. For three months running, my father was unable to pay R' Sender's fee. I came home one day with a letter from the teacher, saying that unless he received his salary by the next morning he would be forced to stop teaching me. When my parents read that letter they were devastated. For them, my Torah education was everything!

"That evening, when my father went to shul, he heard a rich man complaining that the builders who were putting up a new home for his son and new daughter-in-law were unable to find an oven. He offered six rubles to anyone who could find an oven for him. In Russia, an oven was an essential item for the home, used both for heating the house as well as for cooking and baking.

"Returning home, my father discussed the matter with my mother and they agreed on a plan of action. My father would take apart our oven, brick by brick, and build a new one for the rich man. Then they would have six rubles for my teacher.

"The plan was duly carried out. My father received the six rubles and immediately handed them to me. 'Give this to R' Sender,' he instructed me. 'Tell him that three rubles are for payment already owed to him for my Yankel Dovid's tuition, and the other three are for the next three months.'

"That winter was a harsh one. We constantly shivered from the cold — just so that I would have the best teacher and grow up with a good Torah education."

The Ridbaz stopped speaking for a moment before continuing. "It was cold outside this afternoon, and I thought that perhaps I would arrange a *minyan* in my house instead of walking to shul. And then I decided that, in my father's honor, I should make a special effort to go to shul and not *daven* at home.

"When I arrived here a little while ago, I started thinking about my father's sacrifice — my whole family's sacrifice — that bitterly cold winter, for me and my Torah education. That is why I cried. I was remembering my parents' boundless love and devotion, giving up everything so that their child might learn the holy Torah."

Part Thirteen:

Mother of the Yeshivah

❧ In Her Merit

REBBETZIN MICHLA, DAUGHTER OF THE *GAON* R' MEIR
Atlas, Rav of Salant, became the wife of the Torah giant,
R' Elchonon Wasserman. She had an important role to
play in her husband's Torah, as well as that of his students at
the Baranovich Yeshivah. Devotedly she cared for their needs
like a mother.

In the year 5667 (1907) they moved to Radin, where R'
Elchonon wanted to learn in the *kollel* established by his own
rebbe, the Chofetz Chaim. Only three years later, however,
he was asked to serve as *Rosh Yeshivah* in Brisk. Then, with the
outbreak of World War I, there was a general migration
of people out of Brisk. R' Elchonon and his family moved
back to Radin.

The war had reached Radin, too, and the Chofetz Chaim's yeshivah was split in two. One part settled in the city of Smilovitz, and the Chofetz Chaim asked his student, R' Elchonon, to head it.

It was no easy matter in those days to keep a yeshivah going, and the burden of raising funds fell squarely on R' Elchonon's shoulders. As their usual sources of income quickly dried up, hundreds of students were deprived of the barest necessities of life.

In this crisis, Rebbetzin Michla's greatness came to the fore. She undertook to support the yeshivah. Studying the art of soap-making, she turned a significant portion of her home into a soap factory. The work was back breaking, but knowing that the yeshivah boys would be able to eat as a result of her labor made her unstinting in her efforts.

Most of the day and night was spent toiling over her vats of soap. She boiled the fat, shaped the soap bars and packed them in cartons — while continuing to run her home and serve as a substitute mother to each and every one of the yeshivah students. And in the yeshivah, the Torah learning continued. They knew they could rely on the Rebbetzin, whose whole world was built around the sounds of Torah echoing in the streets of Smilovitz. It was this sweet music that lent her the remarkable strength she brought to her self-appointed task: the work of upholding the precious Torah.

A Mother's Heart

R' Yisrael Abuchatzera, the "Baba Sali," was spiritual leader of his yeshivah, but yeshivahs have material requirements as well. "If there is no flour, there is no Torah"; and it was his wife, the Rebbetzin, who took care of all the material needs of the yeshivah.

The Rebbetzin was like a mother to the yeshivah boys, day and night. She cooked their meals, did their laundry and mended their clothing. When they needed new clothes, she sewed them herself. If a new student came who was not dressed suitably, she made sure he was quickly and properly outfitted. Frequently, she gave her own son's clothes to a student who had none of his own. If a student fell ill, she would nurse him back to health with total devotion until he was well enough to return to his studies.

Each student was like a son to her. She knew the boys who lived in town with their parents and those who came from far away. These latter students received the Rebbetzin's special attention. R' Nissim Amsalam, who came to the yeshivah from Algiers, remembers fondly the Rebbetzin's care when he was separated from his parents for an extended period. Often, at mealtimes, she would arrange a second helping of food for him. "Give Nissim another portion," she would say. "He has no place else to eat but here."

When a student reached marriageable age, the Rebbetzin exerted every effort to provide him with all he needed in order to marry — and her joy in his marriage was as great as if he were her own son. Many of the students continued learning at the yeshivah after the wedding. Then, too, the young couple would find her assiduous in seeing to their needs, helping to ease the burden of housekeeping so that the man might be as free as possible for Torah.

And she did all this in addition to running her own considerable and bustling household, which she and her husband kept open day and night to guests, visitors and individuals seeking material and spiritual help. To all of them, the Rebbetzin's heart and hands were as open and giving as any mother's to her beloved children.

❧ The Good Wife

When the *gaon* R' Meir Atlas, rabbi of the city of Shavl departed this world, his flock was left shepherdless. They turned to R' Meir's son-in-law, R' Elchonon Wasserman, to fill his father-in-law's place.

The financial situation in the Wasserman household at that juncture was extremely difficult. This was largely due to R' Elchonon's insistence on taking for himself and his family, out of his yeshivah's budget, only the barest minimum necessary for subsistence. His wife, Rebbetzin Michla, saw the Salant proposal as a heaven-sent opportunity to escape the dire poverty that threatened to engulf her family in Baranovich. Apart from this consideration, she was anxious to be with her widowed mother, who was alone in Salant.

R' Elchonon, however, was adamant in refusing the Salant offer. From the days of his youth, it had always been his custom to steer clear of the rabbinate. At the age of 28 he had been offered the post of chief rabbi of Moscow, and had turned it down. In addition, he had no desire to be separated from his yeshivah at Baranovich.

The matter gnawed at the Rebbetzin, until she decided to travel to the Chofetz Chaim to seek his advice. She readied herself for the journey to Radin, packing her bags and ordering a wagon to carry her and her luggage to the train station.

When the wagon pulled up in front of her house to load the Rebbetzin's bags, she suddenly saw her husband standing in a corner, tears in his eyes. R' Elchonon was afraid that his Rebbe, the Chofetz Chaim, would instruct him to leave his beloved yeshivah and accept the post of rabbi.

Seeing how deeply the issue touched her husband's heart, the Rebbetzin found her own will dissipating. All her calculations were put aside in the face of her husband's wishes. She sent the wagon away and dismissed the whole matter from her mind, never to be raised again.

◆ Priorities

The book *Olam Chesed Yibaneh* (from the *Tikkun HaMiddos* series) presents the following wonderful story about the value of supporting Torah scholars, especially through actual physical work. Special significance is put on giving help through personal labor and devotion — as though one were literally carrying the Torah on his shoulders.

When R' Aryeh Leib Epstein, Rabbi of Koenigsberg and author of *Sefer HaPardes,* passed away in the year 5535 (1775), community leaders met to discuss the selection of a man to fill his place. Their choice fell on the Rabbi of Lokunik who, apart from his reputation as an outstanding *gaon* and *tzaddik,* had always had a deep friendship with their departed Rabbi.

Acting on this decision, the committee wrote up a contract for the Lokunik Rabbi. Two fine Torah scholars were appointed as messengers, charged with the task of bringing the contract to the Rabbi and accompanying him back to Koenigsberg.

The messengers set out in high spirits, confident that the Rabbi of Lokunik would agree to leave his present position in his small town, where he received a weekly salary of two and a half gold coins. The yeshivah in Lokunik had an enrollment of no more than 30 students. In Koenigsberg, the Rabbi would receive 18 gold coins each week, and the yeshivah boasted 200 students, among them several of genius and near-genius caliber. In Koenigsberg, the Rabbi would find a broad field in which to sow his talents and reap superlative fruit — a generation of scholars and *gaonim*.

It was on a Tuesday that the messengers reached Lokunik. They immediately went to the *beis midrash*, where they found the Rabbi and apprised him of their city's offer. The Rabbi read the contract, skimming lightly over those sections pertaining to his salary, as though that information was totally unimportant. When he reached the section detailing the number of students enrolled in the Koenigsberg Yeshivah, and their high level of studies, his eyes lit up. Radiantly, he said, "It will be hard for me to leave my small town, where the people have exerted themselves to the point of real sacrifice in order to support me with honor. Still, I am certain that they can have no complaint against me if I leave them for Koenigsberg, because the yeshivah there is large, enabling me to spread more Torah than I can do here. But I must consult with my wife, the Rebbetzin, and ask for her consent. It is sometimes difficult for a woman to live in a large city."

The Rabbi went home and told the Rebbetzin about the offer. Then he discussed his options with her. It would be difficult to leave his town, where he had formed a close bond to each and every Jew, concerning himself with their needs and praying on their behalf. But what, in the final analysis, was more important than teaching Torah to the multitudes? In Koenigsberg, he would find a much broader scope for his Torah, and by teaching others he would also elevate himself. Moreover, he had heard that the yeshivah students in that city were outstanding. He was convinced that, knowing all this, Lokunik's Jewish community would not stand in his way, especially if he took care to install a fine rabbi in his place.

The Rebbetzin listened attentively to everything her husband said. As the wife of a *tzaddik* and daughter of a Torah scholar, she felt the force of his logic, and agreed to go along with his wishes.

Upon the Rabbi's acceptance of their proposal, the messengers were overjoyed. They decided to remain in town over Shabbos to hear the Rabbi's parting sermon — his farewell to the community. They would travel back to Koenigsberg immediately after Shabbos, bearing the good news that the new rabbi would soon arrive.

This was their intention. But Heaven decreed otherwise.

On Thursday, as the Rebbetzin prepared to wash her laundry in honor of the Shabbos, as was her custom, it suddenly occurred to her that the question of switching rabbinical posts was not that simple. She could not leave Lokunik for Koenigsberg. Here, there was a mitzvah she performed each week with her own hands: washing the yeshivah boys' clothes every Thursday, and mending them where necessary. On Fridays, she would personally distribute a clean shirt to each student. This was a mitzvah she would not be able to perform in the new place.

In the German city of Koenigsberg, the Rebbetzin would sit on her chair like a princess, with a staff of servants to carry out her every command. The Jewish community there would never permit their Rebbetzin to wash the yeshivah boys' laundry with her own hands. And if that was the case, was it really a good idea to leave Lokunik?

Sobs burst from the Rebbetzin as she realized that this might be the last time she would wash the yeshivah's laundry — the last time she could perform this service for young men dedicated, body and soul, to Torah. She decided to bring up the matter with her husband, and ask him to reconsider his decision.

Mustering her courage, she turned to her husband in the presence of the Koenigsberg messengers, and said, "I have changed my mind. I am absolutely unable to leave this town, with its poor *bnei Torah* whom I serve with my own hands, washing and mending their clothes each week."

The messengers were stunned. Coming like a thunderbolt out of the blue, the words caught them by complete surprise.

That Shabbos, the Rabbi did not deliver a parting sermon. On *Motza'ei Shabbos*, he informed the messengers that he could not act against the wishes of his Rebbetzin on a matter that touched her so deeply. The messengers returned to Koenigsberg empty-handed.

Or perhaps, not so empty-handed after all. They brought back with them from Lokunik a new way of thinking about a way of life completely different from the lifestyle they had grown accustomed to in their own large city. The Rebbetzin's words were engraved on their hearts, along with their awe at the fierce spirit that made her so utterly devoted to the welfare of those who serve the Torah.

The following words are inscribed in Lokunik's official archives:

"Thanks to the good and righteous Rebbetzin, our community has merited having our great and righteous Rabbi continue leading our flock for the rest of his days. And even after his death he will not leave us, for his final resting place will be in our soil, so that the holiness and righteousness that influenced us during his lifetime may continue even after death, until the end of days."

✒ "Ima Rachel"

Rebbetzin Rachel Toledano, wife of R' Raphael Baruch Toledano, was known as a woman who loved the Torah and was devoted to those who studied it. This went far beyond her own husband and sons; she was a caring mother to the students who lived in her home for years at a time. Each and every yeshivah student who ate and slept in the Toledano house felt completely at home. If he fell sick, she undertook his complete care until he recovered. If she washed his clothes, she also ironed and mended them as though they belonged to her own children.

The Rebbetzin was always available to her students, even at busy times such as that preceding candle lighting on Friday afternoon. When a student came over and said, *"Senora Rachel, please mend my socks,"* she sat down immediately to mend them, to please the boy and allow him to quickly resume his learning.

For one boy who lived with them, the Toledanos provided regular financial support as well. His father, trying to economize, did not send him a proper allowance. The boy found everything he needed at the Toledanos. After the Rebbetzin passed away, that young man declared, "I received all my *Yiddishkeit*, all my education in Torah and mitzvos, in 'Ima Rachel's' house. Her devotion supported me during the hard times. Without that, who knows where I would be today."

Part Fourteen:

A Torah Home

🐝 On Her Own Shoulders

R' YECHIEL MICHEL HALEVI EPSTEIN WAS A GREAT MAN. He authored the *Aruch HaShulchan*, a commentary on all four sections of the *Shulchan Aruch*, as well as other works, and he served as Rabbi of Novardok. His face was kingly, radiant with wisdom. Renowned for his diligence, he turned down several esteemed positions for fear of detracting from his Torah study.

His wife was R' Epstein's mainstay — supporter and source of encouragement on his journey to greatness. Her love for Torah would never allow her to trouble her husband with the mundane concerns that took up so much of her own time and energy.

When she passed away, her husband eulogized her with the following simple but incredible praise: "For 30 years, she managed a store — and I never even knew where that store was located."

🐾 Mother of Royalty

Rachel Toledano was an indulged daughter. She was born to a wealthy Moroccan family, where every meal was fit for a king, where the furnishings were lavish and her clothing beautiful. There was a staff of servants to tend to every corner of the house.

Her father, R' Shalom Amar, a prominent Rabbi, was a righteous and respected man. After his sudden death at the age of 36, his spirit and love for Torah continued to fill his home. True to her father's precepts, young Rachel grew up with a single burning ambition: to marry a *ben Torah* and establish a Torah home of her own. To one truly devoted to Torah, she would dedicate her every thought and effort.

From the moment she was joyously wed to R' Raphael Baruch, Rachel left behind all the trinkets and indulgences of her childhood and embarked on a life of simplicity. She slept on a straw mattress, in contrast to the soft wool mattress that had been hers in her father's home. Her abode was poor, furnished with the bare minimum, but Rachel was happy. "I don't need a thing," was her constant refrain. She was prepared to sublimate her every need for the sake of Torah.

The formerly wealthy girl never complained about the difficulties of raising her children and managing her home without a single servant. She never asked her husband for help in caring for the children, leaving him free to learn Torah and serve Hashem. When a child woke in the night, she took care that it did not disturb her husband. Though their entire house consisted of one large room, he never heard the babies crying; Rachel slept lightly through the nights, prepared to jump out of bed at the first whimper. Nothing must disrupt her husband's learning. She sacrificed herself totally to Torah, building an awesome spiritual legacy with her own two hands.

Our Sages have said that Hillel (a paragon of what a poor man can achieve in Torah) brought merit upon the poor, while R' Yehudah did the same for the rich. People who knew Rebbetzin Rachel Toledano would quip: "Rachel heaps merit upon rich girls married to *bnei Torah!*"

Her crowning virtue was being satisfied with little. Until his appointment as *Av Beis Din* of Marrakesh, R' Raphael Baruch learned in a *kollel* whose weekly stipend was one *rial* (equivalent to earning about $75 today). This meager sum was not nearly enough to support the family and their steady stream of guests. To supplement it, Rachel worked long hours sewing buttons and beads onto Arab garments. It was backbreaking labor, requiring a special skill and endless patience. She had to borrow money to purchase a sewing machine, working many days just to pay off the loan. Only when the loan was repaid did her earnings begin to help at home, though the family's lifestyle remained restricted to the bare necessities.

In the way of wise women, the Rebbetzin managed to conceal their situation from the public eye. "The hunger," she would say, "is inside. Outside, we are princes." She used leftover scraps or inexpensive fabrics to sew beautiful clothes for her children. She herself dressed in a manner suitable to a respected Torah scholar's wife.

Every spare minute was dedicated to eking out a living. When her husband returned home from the *beis midrash*, she would rise to welcome him and serve him a hot meal. Only after he had retired would she return to her corner where, by candlelight, she would continue sewing quietly while her family slept. She did all this solely to support her husband in his learning and to raise her children in a Torah environment.

Her dedication to this ideal bore wonderful fruit. From the fertile soil she provided, sons and grandsons grew to spread Torah down through the years.

❧ Gratitude

A long line of customers snaked up to the door of a small shop on a narrow street in Radin. Many people preferred shopping at the Chofetz Chaim's store to any other.

They had several good reasons for this. First: It was pleasant to know that a Torah scholar would benefit by their purchases. Also, they could rely implicitly on R' Yisrael Meir's integrity and his scrupulous honesty in weights and measures. So people flocked to the store, which was managed by the Chofetz Chaim's wife. She undertook to support the family so that her husband might dwell in the halls of Torah.

Late each night, when R' Yisrael Meir returned home from the *beis midrash*, his wife would present him with a listing of the inventory and the day's transactions. He would carefully review everything, make the necessary calculations, and return to his Gemara. They continued in this manner for a period of time, until the Chofetz Chaim ascertained that the income the store was earning exceeded their living expenses. From then on, the store hours were shortened, until the shop was open only the amount of time necessary to provide their livelihood.

His good wife never asked her husband to come help in the shop. Her greatest pleasure came from the knowledge that she was making it possible for him to achieve perfection in his Torah and his *avodas Hashem*.

In *Toldos Yemei Chay'av*, a biography of the Chofetz Chaim, his son relates how he often heard the Chofetz Chaim extol his wife's simplicity and her contentment with so little. "For the little Torah that I have, I must thank your mother, who was satisfied even with a dry piece of bread. She didn't demand pretty clothes, beautiful apartments, or the like."

The son went on to tell of the time he went shopping with his mother for clothes to wear at his wedding. As the salesman measured the suit on him, he blessed him: "May you wear it with success, and become a wealthy businessman!" Hearing this, the *chasan's* mother grew enraged: "Who asked you for such a blessing? Bless him that he should be a great *talmid chacham* and have *yiras Shamayim!*"

Without any intention of boasting, the Chofetz Chaim told his son that as a young man, a number of matches involving rich girls were suggested to him. When his brothers got word of his engagement to the girl from Radin, they begged him not to marry her. But marry her he did, and moved to Radin.

"If not for this small town and for everything your mother has done, who knows if I would have attained any Torah? I might have been dragged into the cares of everyday life like so many others my age."

❧ So that He Can Sit and Learn

The Yerushalemski wedding was over, and the joyous seven days of celebration were behind them. The groom was the young genius, R' Yechezkel Abramsky, a name already spoken of with vast respect by all. The bride, Raizel, was ecstatic at her good fortune in marrying a man who was destined to be one of the generation's Torah leaders. Her own love of Torah prompted her to undertake any personal sacrifice that might become necessary in the years to come to promote her husband's spiritual ascendancy.

With his in-laws' support, R' Yechezkel would have no financial worries. But his father-in-law strongly urged him to travel to Brisk, to learn from R' Chaim of Brisk and draw from his boundless well of Torah. It was no simple matter, leaving home so soon after the wedding. Would his wife agree? Was she strong enough in her willingness to sacrifice her own pleasure — including her home life — for the sake of Torah?

R' Yechezkel went to his bride and asked for her consent. Her answer was brave, and extremely encouraging: "Of course," she said at once. "Of course I give my full consent. Should I be the one to keep my husband from greatness?"

R' Yechezkel, accordingly, set out for Brisk. He stayed there for six months, leaving his new wife behind in her parents' home.

When World War I broke out, R' Yechezkel was serving as Rabbi of Slomovitz. The areas bordering on Germany were emptied of Jews, who moved on into Russia. Heading this migration was R' Chaim of Brisk, who moved to the city of Minsk.

An hour's travel now separated R' Yechezkel Abramsky from his rebbe. With his wife's encouragement, he would set out at the beginning of each week for Minsk, remain there for a few days, and return home near the week's end. Rebbetzin Raizel was alone again — alone with her two small children, age 2½ and 6 months. The mother happily took care of her children while her husband, through his learning with his rebbe in Minsk, climbed to ever greater spiritual heights.

Slomovitz suffered greatly during the war, especially after the Communist Revolution and the Polish rebellion against Russia. The town was held in turn by different parties to the struggle. When the Russians took Slomovitz, the Poles rained heavy artillery on the town. When Poland managed to wrest the town from Russia, the Russian army departed, but not before setting off enough bombs to set the whole place aflame. All through this difficult period, R' Yechezkel was in Minsk.

During the bombing, the Rebbetzin's home was burned to the ground. With two babies in her arms and two more at her side, she ran to find more secure shelter. None of her possessions had been spared. She was thrown on the mercy of the townspeople.

When R' Yechezkel heard the news, he returned at once to Slomovitz. He found his wife and children in a public shelter. Even as the members of the Jewish community worked to find them a new place to live, the Rebbetzin told her husband that, as far as she was concerned, he could return to his studies in Minsk. R' Yechezkel did as she asked. Rebbetzin Raizel moved into a new home and managed it alone, serene in the knowledge that she was fulfilling her self-appointed mission: to ensure that no mundane household affair ever be permitted to disturb her husband's rise to heights in Torah.

✌ The Dybbuk

The following story was related by R' Eliyahu HaCohen Dushnitzer, *mashgiach* of Lomza Yeshivah in Petach Tikva, who heard it from a giant of the previous generation, R' Elazar Moshe Hurwitz of Vilna.

R' Nota, a Jewish merchant in Kelm, known to all by the name of Reb Nottel, had an only daughter. She married an outstanding yeshivah student and her father gave the couple a generous dowry and the promise of several years' support.

For three years — the period of his father-in-law's assistance — the young man busied himself with Torah study. When the support ended, his wife came to him complaining, "How will we eat? How will we earn our livelihood? Perhaps we should start a business from which we can earn a living."

The husband replied that he could not separate himself from Torah study.

"Torah study?" the wife repeated. "Naturally, that would be my preference, too. But what can we do? Let's take the dowry money and open a business. I'll stand behind the counter most of the day and you'll come in for just two or three hours. All the rest of the time you can continue learning just as you do now."

The husband considered the plan, and came to the conclusion that, after all, they did need to earn their living; if his wife was willing to take upon herself the lion's share of the burden in running the business, then perhaps that was the right thing to do.

They took the dowry money and opened a business. For the first three months, all went according to plan. The woman worked most of the day, with the husband coming in to take over for two hours, so that she might attend to household matters. But this initial arrangement did not last long. Gradually, the man became more and more involved in the business; the two hours turned to three, then four, and then five, six and eight hours a day. At the end of two years, he was completely immersed in the business — to the point that he forgot to open up a Gemara anymore.

One *Motza'ei Shabbos*, a violent snowstorm raged outside. The wind howled and the snow swirled relentlessly. A little after midnight, the woman went outside to dispose of a barrel of dirty water. As she stepped back indoors, she felt as though she were choking. She could not utter a word. Alarmed, her husband ran to fetch a doctor — but the doctor had no idea what the trouble was.

The next day they went together to consult with other medical experts. No one was able to diagnose the source of the mysterious illness or to prescribe a cure. At last, in desperation, they traveled to Vilna to visit the foremost doctors of their region. It was all in vain.

After all medical causes were ruled out, they began to wonder if perhaps a *dybbuk* had entered the woman. True, R' Chaim Volozhin had written several decades earlier that the state of *hester panim* was so profound that even *dybbuks,* who had been found in previous generations, were unheard of these days. Still, even in present times their symptoms were recognizable, and the couple could not help wondering if this was the source of their trouble. Accompanied by the woman's father, R' Nottel, they traveled to the city of Stuchin, home of the *mekubal*, R' Mendel.

R' Mendel posed a question to the woman. A voice emerged from inside the woman, though her lips were not moving. All present were deeply shaken: "It *is* a *dybbuk*!"

"We don't know that for certain," R' Mendel remonstrated. Turning to the woman, he asked, "Who is with you?" The answer came back: "Five angels of destruction."

"Name them."

When the voice had given the names, R' Mendel said, "It *is* a *dybbuk*. The soul has given the correct names."

It took several more questions to elicit the *dybbuk's* full story. The soul was that of a person who had died 60 years earlier. In his youth, he had lived in Brisk, and traveled from there to Africa, where he fell in with a group of wicked people. It was not long before he was committing all sorts of sins and falling to ever lower levels of decadent behavior. One day, when traveling by wagon, he fell off onto the road and was killed. Ever since, he had been a wandering soul in the world.

"Why did you not do *teshuvah*?" R' Mendel asked.

The *dybbuk* replied that the suddenness and shock of his fall swept all thoughts of repentance from his mind before his death. The unfortunate soul had lost his last chance to repent in his lifetime. Consequently, he had been forced to wander for 60 years among the angels of destruction. It is a kabbalistic precept that, should such a soul succeed in penetrating a living human being, he finds refuge there from the destructive angels, who are prohibited from entering the living. The *dybbuk* did not want to leave its haven.

R' Mendel asked, "Why did you choose to inflict such suffering upon this woman?"

The *dybbuk* burst into raucous laughter. "Both her mother and her husband's mother (both of whom were already in the next world) were clamoring for me to enter her and to cause her this suffering, because she distracted her husband from Torah study. If not for this, she would have no lasting existence either in this world or in the next!"

[At this point, R' Lopian, who also told this story, would add a few words about the *dybbuk's* behavior during this session. The onlookers saw it change form in horrible ways. At times it erupted in awful shrieks, terrified of the destructive angels waiting to tear him to pieces the moment he emerged. Soon after this, the *dybbuk* began spewing a stream of obscenities, until the listeners were forced to cover their ears. R' Mendel asked how it was that he could be screaming in terror at one moment and speaking in such foul and vulgar language at the next. The *dybbuk* replied that the Next World is like this one in that one cannot be cleansed from sin unless one repents. The soul continues to harbor the same evil desires above as he had pursued below, but with a difference: In the Next World there is not the shred of a possibility of attaining any part of what he desires. The suffering he undergoes through desiring that which can never be actualized is truly terrible.]

R' Mendel of Stuchin told the woman's husband to promise to return to Torah study. In addition, his father-in-law, R' Nottel, pledged to learn *mishnayos* for the ascendancy of the unfortunate soul inhabiting his daughter's body, and to donate a sum of money for candles to be lit for that soul in shul. Then R' Mendel gathered a *minyan* of men, seated the woman in a chair in the center of the room and, with the men reciting *Tehillim* and R' Mendel standing behind them, he chanted certain words.

Suddenly, the woman fell off the chair. A powerful voice came from her, crying out, "*Shema Yisrael,*" — so loudly that it was heard all through Stuchin. Then the nail of her little finger flew off and one pane of window glass shattered (as is brought down in *sifrei Kabbalah*). She fell silent.

R' Eliyahu HaCohen Dushnitzer, who related this story to R' Sholom Schwadron, concluded: "You may tell this story to anyone who will listen, especially young people, so that they may understand how important it is to take care never to stray from learning Torah and be strengthened in their own diligence. What I have related I heard from the *gaon* R' Elazar Moshe. I added nothing and exaggerated nothing, and am certainly not telling lies, *chas v'shalom*. You may pass that on to everyone.

"I might add that I know that couple who are now elderly. They live in Tel Aviv, and have a large family, with children and grandchildren. One *Motza'ei Shabbos* I visited them at home and heard this story from their lips, exactly as I have told it to you."

❧ Behind the "Even HaEzel"

Rebbetzin Baila Hinda Meltzer, wife of R' Isser Zalman Meltzer, was a clever woman. It was she who helped her husband to publish his well-known work, the *Even HaEzel*.

One day, as they were sitting at home, she asked R' Isser Zalman, "Why don't you publish a book of your own *chiddushim* (original thoughts on the Torah)?"

"I have no *chiddushim*," he replied, "and nothing to write."

She was amazed. "How can it be that, after so many years of serving as *Rosh Yeshivah*, you have no *chiddushim* to tell?"

"I do have some *chiddushim*," he admitted, "but very few — an item here and an item there. It's not enough for a whole *sefer*."

"In that case," the Rebbetzin insisted, "print what you have — even if it's only a single signature of a few pages. When you come up with additional thoughts, you can print them and add them to the first plate. Over time, you'll have a big book, in terms of both quantity and quality."

R' Isser Zalman listened to his wife's advice, and printed a single plate with his original thoughts on the Torah. After a while, he went on to print another plate, and then another, until he had the entire *Even HaEzel* on the Rambam — a work in several volumes that is highly respected in the Torah world. "It's all in Rebbetzin Baila Hinda's merit," he acknowledges.

In his introduction to the third volume, R' Isser Zalman writes: "I offer a special blessing to my wife, the Rebbetzin, the *eishes chayil*... Baila Hinda, daughter of the rabbi, the *tzaddik*, the generous and famous Shraga Feivel, who has had a large part to play in the first two volumes of this work. Besides her tremendous efforts to guard my health and keep all distractions from me, she also undertook the work involved in publishing these volumes. She encouraged me to print my first book; she raised the money needed to print it in large numbers; and she copied my writings with her own hand in order to pass it on to the printer. She was involved in all stages of the printing and distribution, leaving me free to immerse myself only in composing my *chiddushim* and arranging them for publication. Hashem will repay her in proportion to her efforts ..."

❧ Her Light is Torah

Mrs. Elisheva Schechter had made a decision never to distract her husband from his learning — a decision which took all her considerable strength of character to abide by. The decision had been no empty slogan; it was woven into the very fabric of Elisheva's life. This was a fabric made up of dedication, will power and a single-minded goal. And its crowning glory was her share in her husband's Torah.

She was like a diamond, shining modestly and brightly within the four walls of their home. The diamond shone on Shabbos and on weekdays, in hard times and in good ones. Neither difficulty, nor fatigue, nor the boredom of routine dimmed its radiant glow — the glow of Torah.

Elisheva's every waking moment was imbued with her devotion to her husband's Torah and his spiritual elevation. She was wise enough to understand that great things are built a little at a time, and that even mighty towers begin with tiny grains of sand. The way to greatness lies in taking advantage of every minute. That was the secret. She guarded every minute jealously, so that not even one should be wasted.

With her fierce love of Torah, she invested every moment with importance. Each one must be used for learning. She tried with all her strength to allow her husband to immerse himself in the sea of Torah day and night. The household routines revolved around his learning schedule. Elisheva deeply respected the hard work and perseverance of one who toils long hours over the Torah in the *beis midrash*, and she felt herself honored to have a share in that labor. It was her job to help him progress in every way possible, and to establish an air of reverence for Torah in their home.

Accordingly, she created a veritable paradise for her scholarly husband — conditions under which he might maximize his spiritual potential. She never bothered him with requests connected to the running of the home, happily assuming its entire burden onto her own shoulders. At many different junctures during their life together, her husband offered to help, to take some of the responsibilities of the home from her. Elisheva's answer was: "If I can do it myself, why should you do it? You just continue to learn in peace. If I need help, I will certainly ask for it."

She did not want her husband to spare even the little time it would take to stop at the grocery store, and she began doing her shopping in Haifa at the end of her teaching day there. They had been married some eight years when R' Schechter stepped into the local grocery for the first time — to the gratification of the storekeeper, who had always wanted to meet Rebbetzin Schechter's husband.

True to her early decision, Elisheva trained herself to cope with everything alone. If something in the house broke, she either fixed it herself or called in a repairman. Once, she went over to a neighbor's house to borrow an electric drill. Realizing that she was planning to use the drill herself, the neighbor offered his help.

Her answer was prompt. "If I don't want to ask my own husband to do it, so that he won't take the time away from his learning, why would I ask you?"

One evening, she was speaking to a friend on the phone. It was the end of a long day, and Elisheva was very tired. The phone conversation was a brief chance for her to rest, with one of her children playing at her side. After a while, the child began yawning and asked to be put to bed. Asking her friend to hold on for a minute, Elisheva picked up the child and carried him to his room.

When she returned, her friend asked curiously, "Why didn't you ask your husband to put him to bed?"

"When my husband is busy learning," she answered simply, "that means one thing to me: It's as if he's not home."

These words could only have come from a woman for whom the importance of Torah was etched into her very being!

Neighboring women related that, when they had to be away from home for any reason and left the children in their husbands' charge, Elisheva would promptly offer to watch them at her house, where they could play with her children. She would say, "It's important to me that there be no *bittul Torah* [time wasted from Torah study]. I'd be happy if you could bring the children here. It's no problem!"

One day, Elisheva knocked at a neighbor's door and said, "I heard the sounds of someone learning, all mixed up with children's voices, some of them crying. I understood from this that their mother is not at home. Please, let them come to our house, so that your learning can be better. It will be our pleasure to have them."

And, on another occasion, after a neighbor mentioned that she would be traveling out of town that day, leaving the children in her husband's care, Elisheva knocked on the door just before the start of the afternoon session at the *kollel*. To the astonished husband, she said, "I'll be happy to look after the children for you. Go to the *kollel* in peace."

When the man returned home after *Ma'ariv*, he found his children tucked into bed, having been fed and washed and changed into their pajamas. There was nothing left for him to do but open his Gemara and learn some more.

❧ The Greatest Help

Mrs. Aliza Greenblatt had worked hard all day. She had washed numerous loads of laundry until dusk, and was now preparing to go outside to hang them all up to dry. Wishing to lighten the load for her, her husband, R' Avraham Baruch, offered to help.

Gently, she refused the offer. "I'll hang up the laundry," she said, "while you sit and learn."

Knowing how hard the work was for her, he insisted on lending a hand. Once again, more forcefully this time, she refused — at one point setting down the heavy basket as though she were not going to hang up the laundry at all. When her husband saw this, he gave up and went back to his learning.

Mrs. Greenblatt quietly hung up the clothes, placing them all along the yard in such a way that her husband would not see her and become distracted from his learning. The knowledge that her own hard work was enabling him to pore over his Gemara was all the reward she needed or wanted.

🐝 Peace of Mind

When Rebbetzin Chaya Sheina Elyashiv passed away, thousands of stories began to circulate about her — about how she had stood behind a husband who was a Torah leader, and behind sons and sons-in-law great in Torah. The central theme running through these anecdotes was her tremendous concern that her husband have the peace of mind to immerse himself in Torah without any other cares.

The Rebbetzin would refrain from telling her husband when one of the children was ill, and kept her own pains and griefs to herself as well, fearing they would trouble his mind which was fully absorbed in Torah. Once, when her father, R' Aryeh Levine, paid her a visit, he noticed that she was setting the table for her husband's supper in her small kitchen. Asking the reason for this unusual behavior, she replied that the children were not well, and were resting in the living room/dining room. She did not want him to eat there, where the sight of the children might disturb him and keep him from learning.

She went to the hospital to give birth 10 times, never once asking her husband to come visit her there. She only wanted him to learn. When R' Yehuda Ze'ev Segal, *Rosh Yeshivah* in Manchester, visited their home, she asked him to give her husband a *berachah*.

"What can I bless Rav Elyashiv with?" he wanted to know.

"That he will make great strides in his learning," she answered. This was the request of a woman nearly 80 years old, near the end of her life.

Her self-sacrifice for the sake of keeping her husband free of any worries was boundless. She dealt with the most difficult situations with courage and ingenuity, rather than disturb her husband's learning.

One of her children was once doubled over with stomach cramps. A doctor, hastily summoned to their home, pronounced the need for immediate surgery. Rav Elyashiv was in the *beis midrash*. "Should someone be sent to fetch him?" she was asked.

"*Chas v'chalilah!*" the Rebbetzin answered firmly. She went alone to the hospital, certain that the merit of her husband's learning would help more than anything. It was only when Rav Elyashiv returned home that evening that he heard that his son had undergone surgery that day.

In the days before Pesach, Jewish homes are traditionally topsy-turvy. The Rebbetzin was apprehensive that the disorder would disrupt her husband's learning whenever he was home, and that his mealtimes would be thrown off schedule. With great difficulty, she saved up her pennies for a lofty goal: to send her husband to a health spa during those hectic days. He was able to learn in peace there, and he returned in time for *bedikas chametz* to find the house sparkling and ready.

Even when the Rebbetzin herself was not feeling well, she refused to trouble her husband. During her last days, when she suffered with her final illness, a granddaughter who stayed at her side through the nights noticed that the Rebbetzin was making every effort to suppress her coughing. She succeeded for two solid hours. When it became impossible to continue, the Rebbetzin went out onto the balcony and coughed there. All this, so that her husband would not awaken from the noise of her coughing.

This was the pattern of their life together. On the morning after their wedding, he went to the *beis midrash* and learned with great diligence. Nothing, through the years, was ever permitted to disturb his concentration or arrest his steady upward climb to spiritual greatness. And when they came to inform him that his Rebbetzin had passed away, he sat in his usual chair, learning with the same diligence. The circle of perfection was complete.

❧ Sources

This volume is part of
THE ARTSCROLL SERIES®
an ongoing project of
translations, commentaries and expositions
on Scripture, Mishnah, Talmud, Halachah,
liturgy, history, the classic Rabbinic writings,
biographies and thought.

For a brochure of current publications
visit your local Hebrew bookseller
or contact the publisher:

Mesorah Publications, ltd

4401 Second Avenue
Brooklyn, New York 11232
(718) 921-9000
www.artscroll.com